Upper Columbia Basin Network
Integrated Water Quality Annual Report 2009

Big Hole National Battlefield (BIHO)

UPPER COLUMBIA
BASIN NETWORK
UCBN

Natural Resource Technical Report NPS/UCBN/NRTR—2010/291

Eric N. Starkey
Aquatic Biologist
Upper Columbia Basin Network- Inventory and Monitoring Program
105 E. 2nd St.
Suite #7
Moscow, ID 83843

February 2010

U.S. Department of the Interior
National Park Service
Natural Resource Program Center
Fort Collins, Colorado

The National Park Service, Natural Resource Program Center publishes a range of reports that address natural resource topics of interest and applicability to a broad audience in the National Park Service and others in natural resource management, including scientists, conservation and environmental constituencies, and the public.

The Natural Resource Technical Report Series is used to disseminate results of scientific studies in the physical, biological, and social sciences for both the advancement of science and the achievement of the National Park Service mission. The series provides contributors with a forum for displaying comprehensive data that are often deleted from journals because of page limitations.

All manuscripts in the series receive the appropriate level of peer review to ensure that the information is scientifically credible, technically accurate, appropriately written for the intended audience, and designed and published in a professional manner. Data in this report were collected and analyzed using methods based on established, peer-reviewed protocols and were analyzed and interpreted within the guidelines of the protocols.

Views, statements, findings, conclusions, recommendations, and data in this report are those of the author(s) and do not necessarily reflect views and policies of the National Park Service, U.S. Department of the Interior. Mention of trade names or commercial products does not constitute endorsement or recommendation for use by the National Park Service.

This report is also available from the Upper Columbia Basin Network (http://www.nature.nps.gov/im/units/UCBN) and the Natural Resource Publication Management website (http://www.nature.nps.gov/publications/NRPM) on the internet.

Please cite this publication as:

Starkey, E. N. 2010. Upper Columbia Basin Network integrated water quality annual report 2009: Big Hole National Battlefield (BIHO). Natural Resource Technical Report NPS/UCBN/NRTR—2010/291. National Park Service, Fort Collins, Colorado.

NPS 341/101187, February 2010

Contents

Figures

Tables

Appendices

Executive Summary

The mission of the National Park Service is "to conserve unimpaired the natural and cultural resources and values of the national park system for the enjoyment of this and future generations" (NPS 1999). To uphold this goal, the Director of the NPS approved the Natural Resource Challenge to encourage national parks to focus on the preservation of the nation's natural heritage through science, natural resource inventories, and expanded resource monitoring (NPS 1999). Through the Challenge, 270 parks in the national park system were organized into 32 inventory and monitoring networks.

The Upper Columbia Basin Network (UCBN) has identified 14 priority park vital signs, indicators of ecosystem health, which represent a broad suite of ecological phenomena operating across multiple temporal and spatial scales. The intent of the network, is to monitor a balanced and integrated "package" of vital signs that meets the needs of current park management, but will also be able to accommodate unanticipated environmental conditions in the future. Water quality is a particularly high priority vital sign for six of the nine UCBN parks. The UCBN contains more than 34 rivers, streams, ponds, and reservoirs located in nine park units spread over four large western states. Unlike many National Parks that are large and often encompass entire watersheds, most UCBN parks and water bodies are small and embedded in large watersheds with diverse land use.

This annual report details the status of key indicators of water quality obtained from the first season of monitoring in Big Hole National Battlefield (BIHO), 2009. Note that several of the appendices in this report are primarily intended for UCBN internal reference. In addition, some appendices serve has hard copies of quality assurance/quality control procedures performed during data processing. Data from the 2009 field sampling effort was collected following methods detailed in the UCBN integrated water quality monitoring protocol (Starkey et al. 2009). The UCBN Integrated Water Quality Monitoring Protocol was formally peer-reviewed and approved for implementation in August 2009. This protocol can be found on the UCBN website at: http://science.nature.nps.gov/im/units/ucbn/reports/index.cfm#IWQ_Mon

Water chemistry and macroinvertebrate results indicate that the North Fork Big Hole River is in good condition, with the primary concerns being dissolved oxygen content below the established TMDL and elevated water temperatures. The status of water quality for the North Fork Big Hole River relative to state regulatory thresholds is given in the summary table on the following page.

UCBN water quality monitoring is conducted on a 3 year rotating panel. As a result, conditions in the North Fork Big Hole River will be re-evaluated in 2012.

North Fork Big Hole River (BIHO) Water Chemistry Summary 2009

Measure	Condition (June-October, 2009)	State DEQ Thresholds
Temperature	* MDMT= 19.06 °C ** MDAT= 17.10 °C	"A 1 °F [0.56 °C] maximum increase above naturally occurring water temperature is allowed"
Specific Conductance (mean)	54.5 µS/cm	N/A
Dissolved Oxygen (mean daily min)	7.37 mg/L	Daily minimum > 8.0 mg/L; 7-d mean > 9.5 mg/L
pH (mean daily max)	7.37 pH Units	6.5-8.5; < 0.5 unit human induced change; Maintain >7.0 if naturally > 7.0
pH (mean daily min)	7.14 pH Units	6.5-8.5; < 0.5 unit human induced change; Maintain >7.0 if naturally > 7.0
Turbidity (mean daily max)	18.8 NTU	"No increase above natural turbidity is allowed"

*MDMT – Maximum Daily Maximum Temperature **MDAT – Maximum Daily Average Temperature

Acknowledgments

Funding for this project was provided through the National Park Service Natural Resource Challenge and the Servicewide Inventory and Monitoring Program. We thank Steve Black and Jim Stone of BIHO for accommodations in park housing during field work. We also thank Jason Lyon and Jimmer Stevenson for their assistance in establishing monitoring locations.

Introduction and Background

Water resources have been identified as a high priority vital sign for the UCBN. These resources are used by many riparian, migratory, and terrestrial organisms in the Network, and have intrinsic value as places of natural beauty and recreation (Garrett et al. 2007). Reflecting this priority, the Water Resources Division (WRD) of the NPS provides a separate source of funding each fiscal year to the Upper Columbia Basin Network (UCBN) to accomplish water quality monitoring. In June 2009 the UCBN began its first year of integrated water quality monitoring in the North Fork Big Hole River at Big Hole National Battlefield (BIHO).

Water resources in the semi-arid west have been strongly affected by human activity, and all UCBN streams and rivers are listed by states as impaired for one or more parameters. Most UCBN water bodies and many aquatic resources such as migratory fish are strongly influenced by activities in the larger watersheds outside park boundaries. Understanding the current status of freshwater ecosystems will help guide management and restoration efforts, and provide insight into ecosystem change in a landscape with a shifting climate and dynamic human influences.

During the process of prioritizing vital signs to monitor in UCBN parks in 2005, water quality was identified as a high priority vital sign (Garrett et al. 2007). When asked what aspects of water quality were important to monitor, resource managers identified the sampling of macroinvertebrate assemblages within UCBN water bodies as the top water quality monitoring priority. Secondary priorities included baseline sampling of water chemistry parameters, characterization of channel morphology, and information on water quantity. Channel morphology and riparian vegetation will be addressed in separate monitoring protocols which are under development.

The foci of the UCBN Integrated Water Quality Monitoring Protocol are aquatic macroinvertebrate assemblage composition and water chemistry. Aquatic macroinvertebrate assemblages have strong effects on freshwater ecosystem processes and represent an important trophic linkage between primary producers and fishes. Measures of macroinvertebrate assemblage composition and structure have been frequently used as water quality indicators because these assemblages integrate the effects of point and non-point source pollutants over spatial-temporal scales and can be used to answer many management questions. Also, macroinvertebrates are more cost-effective to sample than other biota or many water chemistry parameters.

Water chemistry and temperature have strong effects on aquatic biota. Consequently, direct and indirect human alteration of stream water quality is associated with altered biotic communities and ecosystem processes. Because of the direct relationship between water chemistry and biota, water chemistry is typically a central component of any water quality monitoring program. More recently, monitoring of stream water temperatures has increased in the Pacific Northwest, because of concerns over cold-water fish habitat (primarily salmonid fishes), the recognized influence of land- and water-use on stream temperature regime, and the need for baseline temperature information to monitor the effects of climate change. National Park Service (NPS) Water Resource Division (WRD) has identified a suite of four "core water quality parameters", temperature, specific conductance, pH, and dissolved oxygen, which are critical to understanding baseline conditions in aquatic habitats. The UCBN added turbidity as a parameter to measure because turbidity is listed as a source of impairment in several UCBN park streams.

Well articulated desired future condition statements have not yet been developed for water quality in UCBN parks. However, the mission statements for the NPS as a whole and for the individual parks clearly state the intent "to conserve unimpaired the natural and cultural resources and values of the national park system for the enjoyment of this and future generations" (NPS 1999). Water quality is a particularly important resource with nationally recognized merit. It is assumed that desired future conditions for all UCBN parks will include clean streams, rivers, and lakes free of human health concerns that provide visitors with recreational and scenic experiences. Monitoring macroinvertebrate assemblage composition and structure, and core water quality parameters, will directly measure the water characteristics most important to park mission, visitor experience, and desired future conditions.

Objectives

The overarching programmatic goal of the UCBN integrated water quality monitoring program is to obtain information that will aid in informed management decisions pertaining to improved water quality within UCBN parks. Park managers have committed to improving the water quality of impaired waters by adopting the NPS Government Performance Results Act (GPRA) goal that 99.3% of streams and rivers managed by NPS will meet State and Federal water quality standards. Most UCBN waters do not meet standards and are listed on EPA 303(d) lists.

Given the lack of available data on water quality in UCBN parks, the following fundamental questions drive much of the UCBN's inquiry into water quality:

- Are the core water quality parameters of streams in the UCBN with established Total Maximum Daily Loads (TMDLs) selected for sampling improving over time?
- What is the status and long-term trend of core water quality parameters (temperature, pH, conductivity, dissolved oxygen, and turbidity) in UCBN streams selected for sampling?
- What is the status and long term trend in aquatic macroinvertebrate abundance and assemblage composition in selected UCBN streams?
- Do aquatic macroinvertebrate assemblages sampled within UCBN streams indicate polluted or otherwise impaired water quality?
- Do aquatic macroinvertebrate assemblages sampled within UCBN streams indicate "pristine" or "reference" conditions according to regional criteria established by EPA and the states of Idaho, Oregon, Montana, and Washington?

In light of these questions and the broader goals outlined above, water quality monitoring in the UCBN addresses the following specific measurable monitoring objectives:

- Determine status and long term trend in key water quality parameters for selected streams within UCBN park units.
- Determine status and trend in aquatic macroinvertebrate abundance, assemblage composition, and functional feeding group composition in wadeable streams within the UCBN.

Methods

Water Chemistry

A continuous water quality monitor (HACH, MS5 Hydrolab) was deployed in a location that was representative of conditions in the park, logistically feasible to access, and relatively secure from vandalism and high flows. A cross-section survey was conducted to aid in the determination of Hydrolab site selection. A continuous water quality monitor was deployed from June 22nd to October 6th at an index site to estimate the status, variability, and long-term trends in core parameter values at diel, seasonal, annual, and eventually, decadal time scales. The core parameters measured were water temperature, dissolved oxygen, pH, specific conductance, and turbidity. These core parameters were measured hourly and the instrument serviced monthly throughout the deployment period. For more information on the UCBN water chemistry sampling design see Starkey et al. (2009). It should be noted that monitoring occurred from June 22nd to July 27th with a Hydrolab on loan from the Hach Company while Hydrolab 064 was repaired. The loaner Hydrolab was subsequently replaced by the repaired instrument (064). QA/QC information for each Hydrolab is detailed in Appendix E.

Discharge

No USGS gaging station exists on the North Fork Big Hole River or its tributaries. The closest gage is on the Big Hole River near Wisdom MT (USGS 06024540 Big Hole River bl Mudd Cr nr Wisdom MT) and is marginally useful for determining flow in north fork. As a result, no discharge data or results are presented in this report.

Macroinvertebrates

Macroinvertebrates were sampled using protocols established by the Environmental Protection Agency (EPA) Environmental Monitoring and Assessment Program (EMAP) (Peck et al. 2006). The EMAP protocol specifies that sample reach length is determined by the wetted width of the stream. Thereby the number of sample reaches in a park was a function of reach length. The North Fork Big Hole River (BIHO) contained 6 EMAP style reaches. Each sample reach included 11 transects that were permanently marked on the left bank. Macroinvertebrate samples were taken at each transect with a D-frame kick net and composited as a single sample for each reach. For more information on the UCBN macroinvertebrate sampling design see Starkey et al. (2009).

Coliform

At the request of the park, coliform samples were collected to determine baseline counts for total coliform and fecal coliform. Note that coliform sampling is not routinely performed as part of the Integrated Water Quality Protocol. One sample was taken downstream of the bridge on the North Fork Big Hole River (downstream of the parking lot) September 1st, 2009 and again on October 7th, 2009. Another sample was taken at the confluence of Ruby and Trail Creeks in October 2009. Sample methods were in accordance with guidance given by the Missoula City/County Health Department. All samples were transported to the Missoula City/County Health Department and evaluated using the Quanti-Tray method. For more information see the Missoula county health department website http://www.co.missoula.mt.us/envhealth/WaterLab/24Test.htm (accessed on 10/27/2009).

Study Area

North Fork Big Hole River - Big Hole National Battlefield (BIHO)

The North Fork Big Hole River is in the Big Hole River drainage in Hydrologic Unit 1002000406 (United States Geologic Survey [USGS]), in Beaverhead County, Montana (Figure 2). The drainage area above the park is approximately 241 square km (150 square miles) and consists of several land cover types (NPS 1997). The 3 primary land cover types for BIHO as determined from the National Land Cover Dataset and the National Park Service digital park unit layer include grasslands/herbaceous (32%), evergreen forest (23%), and woody wetland (21%) (Garrett et al. 2007). This is an accurate reflection of land cover types in the North Fork Big Hole River drainage. The confluence of Trail and Ruby Creeks, forming the North Fork Big Hole River, is on the south west boundary of the park. High water in May 2009 prevented water chemistry monitoring prior to mid June.

Threats to water resources in BIHO have been listed as: flow impairment, mining, agriculture, and stormwater runoff (Garrett et al. 2007). In addition, North Fork Big Hole River is listed as impaired in the following areas based on 303(d) criteria: flow impairment and dewatering (Garrett et al. 2007). Designated state beneficial uses are Class A-1 which includes; Cold Water Fishery (CWF), Primary Contact Recreation (PCR), and Aquatic Life (AQL).

The macroinvertebrate sample reaches extended from 300 m downstream of the parking lot to the northern most park boundary (Appendix A). Sample reach 006 is shown in Figure 1. The Hydrolab was deployed approximately 100 meters upstream from the bridge over the North Fork Big Hole River and 40m west of the parking lot. This location was chosen due to logistical considerations and adequate water depth. In addition, the Hydrolab deployment location was chosen to avoid placement of equipment near the culturally significant encampment area.

Figure 1. North Fork Big Hole River looking upstream from transect F, sample reach 006, during macroinvertebrate sampling on July 28nd 2009.

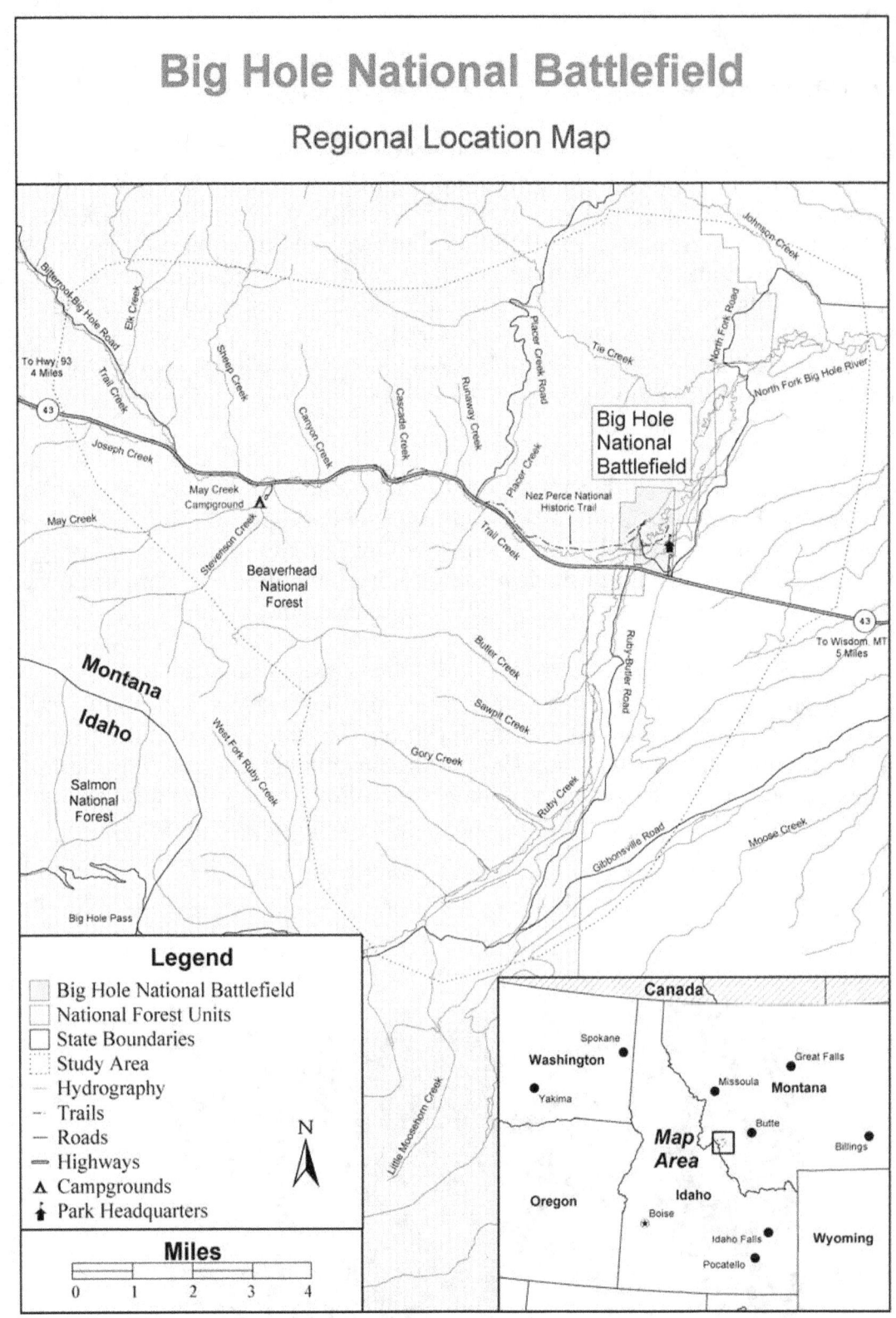

Figure 2. Big Hole National Battlefield regional map (NPS 1997).

6

Results and Discussion

Water Chemistry:

Cross Section Survey:

A cross section survey was conducted at the proposed multiprobe deployment location to evaluate if the site was reasonably representative of stream conditions throughout the park. As suggested by the water resource division the UCBN will judge overall representativeness primarily on the basis of specific conductance (Starkey et al. 2009). It should be noted that transects 1-4 of the cross section survey were placed downstream from the monitoring location. Typically, transects are placed upstream, however at BIHO there was not adequate stream length above the proposed monitoring location to accommodate 4 transects.

The 2009 deployment location provided adequate water depth throughout the field season, was easily accessible, and was outside of culturally significant areas. Other locations were unfeasible for continuous monitoring and installation of monitoring equipment.

An analysis of variance (ANOVA) test was conducted to evaluate representativeness (SPSS v16.0). Results of the ANOVA showed that there was no significant difference for specific conductance among the transects and the deployment location in July $F_{(4,45)}=1.719$, $p = 0.162$ and a significant difference in October $F_{(4,42)}= 3.196$, $p = 0.022$.

To determine where the difference in representativeness occurred, a post hoc Tukey's was conducted (SPSS v16.0). Relative to specific conductance, results of the Tukey's test for the cross section conducted in November indicate that the deployment location was not significantly different from each of the 4 downstream transects, but rather that there was a significant difference between transects 1 and 4.

In summary, the deployment location was judged to be representative of the entire sample reach.

Quality Assurance/Quality Control (QA/QC):

Quality assurance and quality control for multiprobe data collection are covered in detail in SOP #12 (Starkey et al. 2009). Basic procedures adhere to the guidelines established in Part B lite QA/QC Review Checklist for Aquatic Vital Sign Monitoring Protocols and SOPs (Irwin 2008); the National Coastal Assessment Quality Assurance Project Plan 2001-2004 (U.S. EPA 2001); the Laboratory Methods Manual-Estuaries, Volume 1: Biological and Physical Analyses (U.S. EPA 1995); and Rapid Bioassessment Protocols for Use in Streams and Wadeable Rivers (Barbour et al. 1999).

General quality assurance and quality control methods for UCBN water quality multiprobe calibration and data downloads include the following:

- Representative multiprobe sample locations are determined by using a cross-section and stream segment survey. Each site is re-assessed for representativeness at the start and end each sample year.

- The UCBN follows pre-established maximum acceptable differences for field instrument calibration and QC checks. If the multiprobe has readings outside of the maximum acceptable differences the multiprobe will likely need to be removed for non-routine maintenance.

- When calibrating the multiprobe, values of known standard solutions will be determined pre and post calibration, to help determine if the instruments measurements have "drifted." In addition, repeated measures of these solutions will help determine the repeatability of multiprobe measures.

- All multiprobe data will be visually checked for outliers and QC issues immediately following the download of data.

- Quantitative and qualitative terms that describe how good data need to be in order to meet project objectives are discussed in detail in SOP #12 Starkey et al. 2009 and Appendix E in this report. NPS WRD lists the following data quality objectives as necessary for water chemistry data: target population, representativeness, completeness, data comparability, measurement sensitivity and detection limits, measurement precision as repeatability, and measurement systematic error/bias.

More detailed QA/QC for water quality multiprobes is contained in SOP #6 and 12, Starkey et al. 2009.

Status:

Condition of core water quality parameters along with the corresponding state Department of Environmental Quality (DEQ) regulatory threshold are given in Table 1. The primary concern is low dissolved oxygen content possibly associated with elevated water temperatures. In most cases, the lowest dissolved oxygen content coincided with elevated water temperatures. Elevated turbidity was due to large rain events on the area that burned during the May Creek fire in 2008 and the Rat Creek fire in 2007. Turbidity levels were likely elevated over the long term average. Each parameter is discussed in further detail below.

Table 1. Vital sign summary table for water chemistry in North Fork Big Hole River June-October, 2009.

North Fork Big Hole River (BIHO) Water Chemistry Summary 2009		
Measure	Condition (June-October, 2009)	State DEQ Thresholds
Temperature	* MDMT= 19.06 °C ** MDAT= 17.10 °C	"A 1 °F [0.56 °C] maximum increase above naturally occurring water temperature is allowed"
Specific Conductance (mean)	54.5 µS/cm	N/A
Dissolved Oxygen (mean daily min)	7.37 mg/L	Daily minimum > 8.0 mg/L; 7-d mean > 9.5 mg/L
pH (mean daily max)	7.37 pH Units	6.5-8.5; < 0.5 unit human induced change; Maintain >7.0 if naturally > 7.0
pH (mean daily min)	7.14 pH Units	6.5-8.5; < 0.5 unit human induced change; Maintain >7.0 if naturally > 7.0
Turbidity (mean daily max)	18.8 NTU	"No increase above natural turbidity is allowed"

*MDMT – Maximum Daily Maximum Temperature **MDAT – Maximum Daily Average Temperature

- Temperature:
  The maximum daily maximum temperature (MDMT) (19.06 °C) is below the regulatory thresholds for many of the streams in the UCBN (20-22 °C). However, given the lack of historic data, comparisons to the existing regulatory threshold for the North Fork Big Hole River are limited. The MDMT was 2°C above the maximum temperature observed by NPS Water Resource Division during their assessment of baseline water quality data in the North Fork Big Hole drainage (NPS 1997). Figure 3 shows the daily maximum and mean temperatures in North Fork Big Hole River from June-October 2009. Figure 4 shows the data rating/grade for each deployment period (monthly interval). These standard USGS ratings are based on the degree of sensor fouling and drift encountered during each deployment period (Wagner et al. 2006; Starkey et al. 2009).

Water temperatures are of particular interest in the North Fork Big Hole River, given that it is considered potential habitat for fluvial Arctic Grayling (*Thymallus arcticus*). Elevated water temperatures can be caused by poor stream shading and dewatering. It is important to note that elevated water temperatures have the capacity to reduce the total concentration of dissolved oxygen (i.e., there is an inverse relationship between water temperature and dissolved oxygen; Figure 7), thereby impacting aquatic biota. Implications of elevated water temperatures may include decreased salmonid recruitment, decreased salmonid health, and potential shifts in fish and benthic macroinvertebrate communities (Vannote and Sweeney 1980; McCullough 1999).

Maintaining water temperatures suitable for naturally occurring species in the North Fork Big Hole River will depend on riparian condition and reduced dewatering basin wide. For this reason cooperation with other agencies, stakeholders, and adjacent landowners will be critical.

- Specific Conductance:
  Specific conductance ranged from 40.79 to 69.06 μS/cm, with an average specific conductance of 54.52 μS/cm. There is no regulatory threshold for specific conductance as it varies widely depending on the geology of the drainage basin and stream discharge. The sudden increase in specific conductance seen in late July-early August was due to suspended materials in the water column (Figure 5). This sudden increase was caused by a large rain event upstream on a recently burned area (the May Creek fire in 2008 and the Rat Creek fire in 2007). Figure 6 shows the data rating/grade for each deployment period (monthly interval). These standard USGS ratings are based on the degree of sensor fouling and drift encountered during each deployment period (Wagner et al. 2006; Starkey et al. 2009). Specific conductance data grades less than excellent were due to a combination of fouling and sensor drift.

Corrections that have been applied to the specific conductance data are listed in Appendix F.

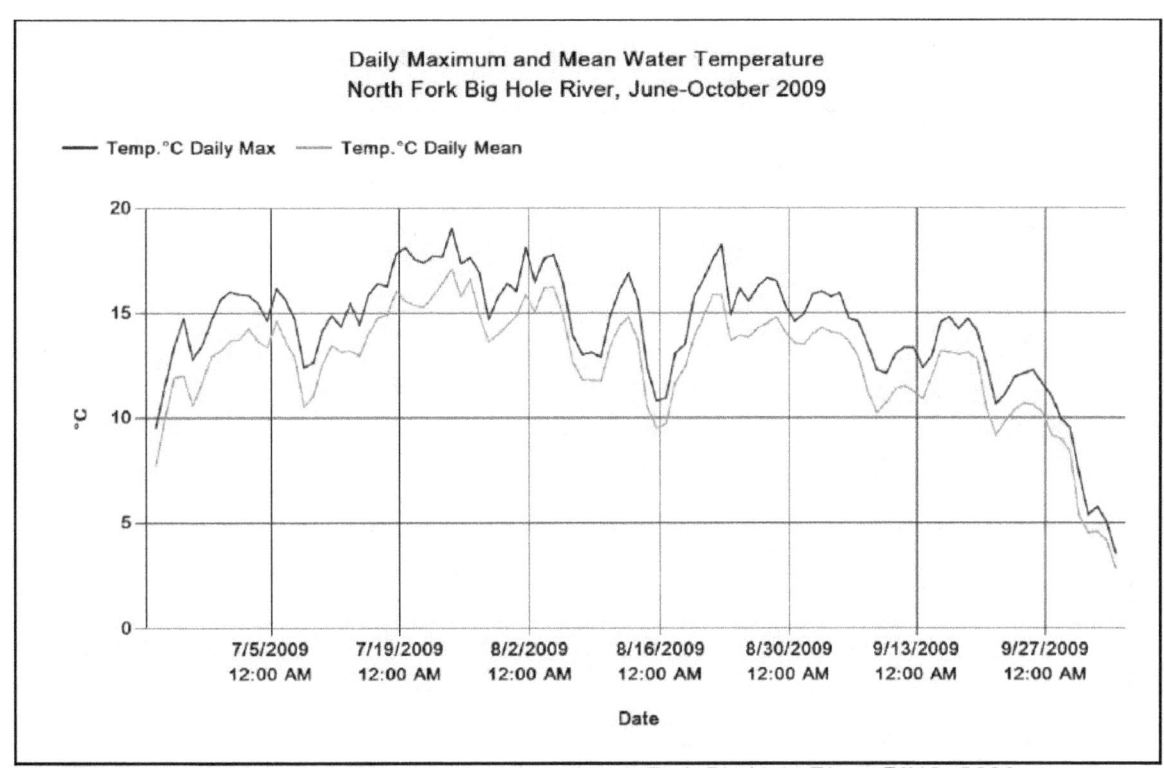

Figure 3. Daily maximum and mean temperature in North Fork Big Hole River, BIHO, 2009.

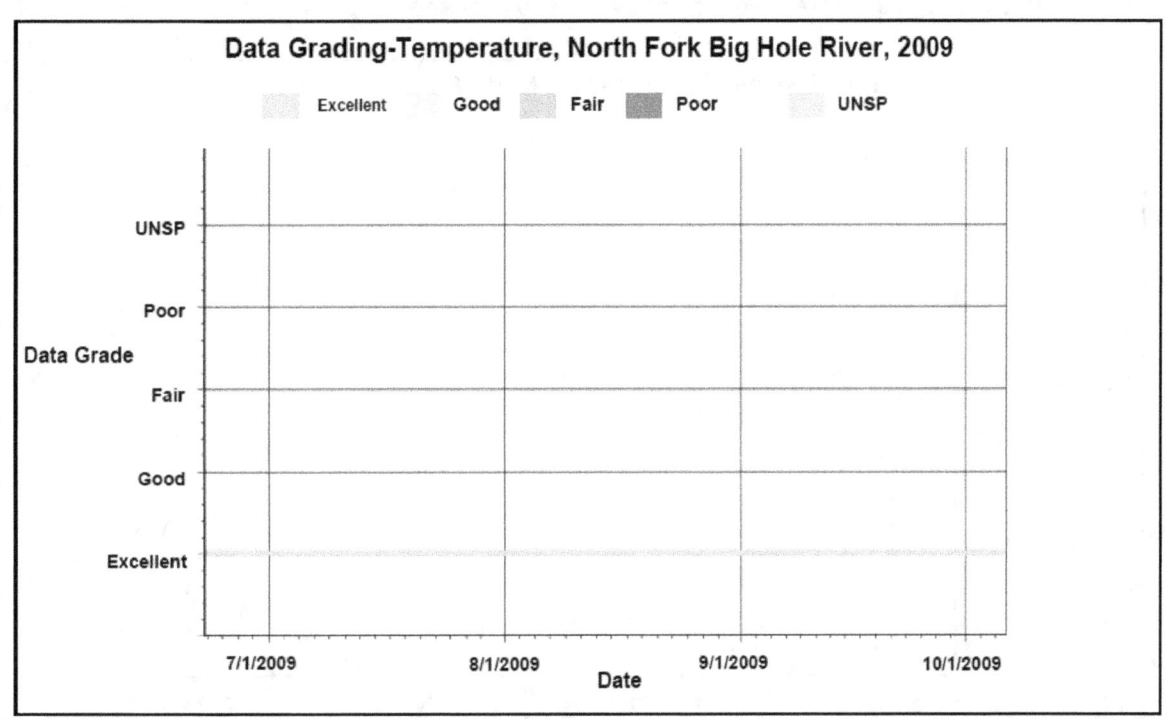

Figure 4. Data grade/rating for temperature each deployment period June-October in North Fork Big Hole River, BIHO, 2009.

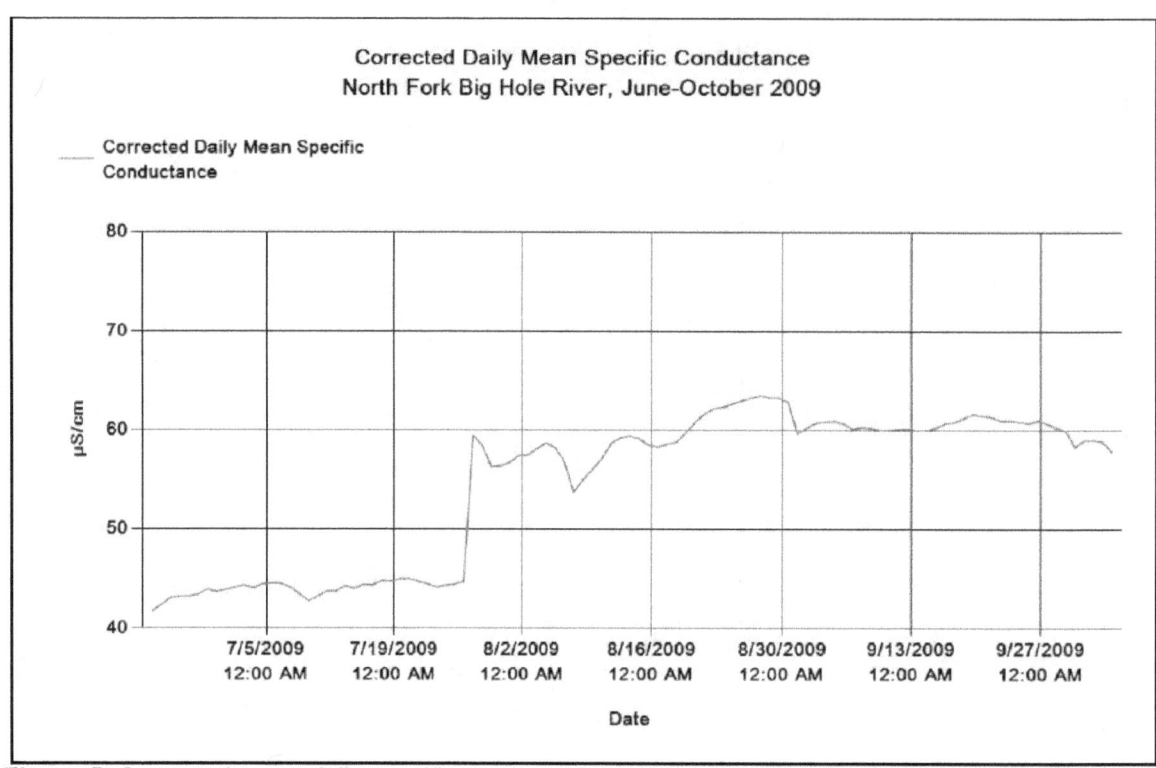

Figure 5. Corrected mean daily specific conductance and mean daily discharge in North Fork Big Hole River, BIHO, 2009. There is no regulatory threshold for specific conductance.

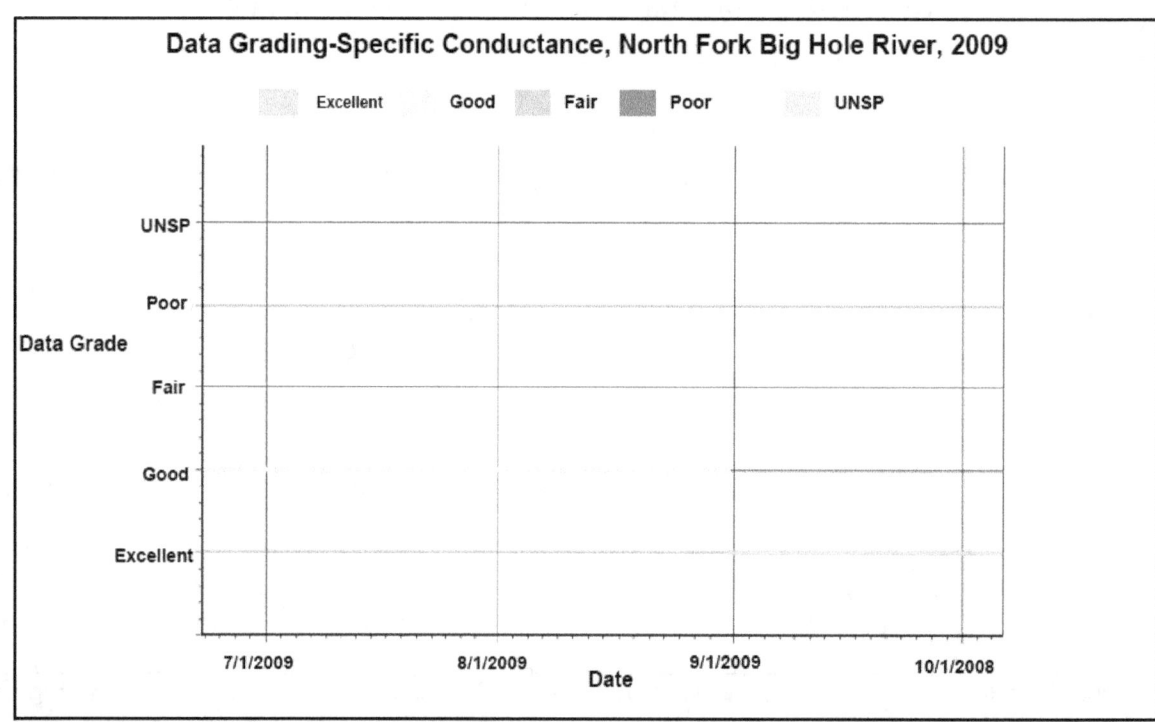

Figure 6. Data grade/rating for specific conductance each deployment period June-October in North Fork Big Hole River, BIHO, 2009. Note that a data grade of "good" was due to a combination of fouling and drift.

12

- Dissolved Oxygen:
  Mean daily minimum dissolved oxygen was 7.37 mg/L and dipped below the regulatory threshold (8.0 mg/L) on 97 of the 106 monitoring days. As expected, low dissolved oxygen levels generally corresponded to spikes in water temperature. Figure 7 shows the daily minimum dissolved oxygen and maximum temperatures in North Fork Big Hole River from June-October 2009. Figure 8 shows the data rating/grade for each deployment period (monthly interval). These standard USGS ratings are based on the degree of sensor fouling and drift encountered during each deployment period (Wagner et al. 2006; Starkey et al. 2009). "Excellent" data grades were attributed to minimal fouling and sensor drift. Corrections that have been applied to the dissolved oxygen data are listed in Appendix F.

  While the North Fork Big Hole River is not on the 303(d) list for dissolved oxygen impairment our monitoring suggests that the North Fork Big Hole River was below the TMDL established by Montana DEQ most of the sample period. Given that dissolved oxygen levels were consistently below 8.0 mg/l elevated temperatures may be depressing dissolved oxygen concentrations. In general, if water temperature was reduced via stream shading or instream flow was greater (reduced dewatering) it is likely that the North Fork Big Hole River would not have dissolved oxygen levels below 8.0 mg/l. The NPS Baseline Water Quality Data Inventory and Analysis (NPS 1997) found that mean dissolved oxygen levels ranged from 8.4 to 9.9 mg/l in tributaries to the North Fork Big Hole River. This suggests that the established TMDL is an appropriate target for the North Fork Big Hole River. Increasing dissolved oxygen will require basin wide riparian and in stream flow improvements and cooperation with other agencies, stakeholders, and adjacent landowners.

- pH:
  The minimum and maximum pH (6.58 and 7.72 respectively) were never outside the acceptable regulatory thresholds of 6.5-8.5 pH units and the mean (7.24 pH units) was well within this range. Figure 9 shows the daily maximum, minimum, and mean pH in the North Fork Big Hole River from June-October 2009. Figure 10 shows the data rating/grade for each deployment period (monthly interval). These standard USGS ratings are based on the degree of sensor fouling and drift encountered during each deployment period (Wagner et al. 2006; Starkey et al. 2009). Data grades less than excellent were due primarily to fouling. Corrections that have been applied to the pH data are listed in Appendix F.

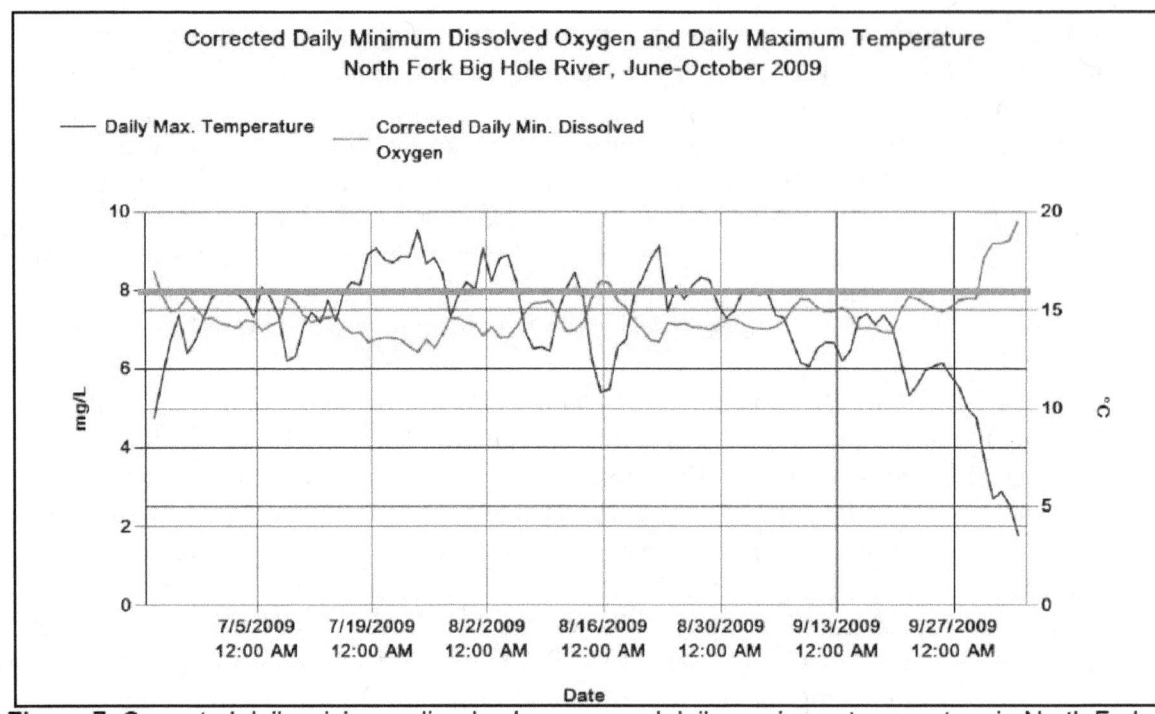

Figure 7. Corrected daily minimum dissolved oxygen and daily maximum temperature in North Fork Big Hole River, BIHO, 2009. The horizontal red line denotes the state DEQ regulatory threshold for daily minimum dissolved oxygen (Daily minimum >8.0 mg/L, 7-day mean >9.5).

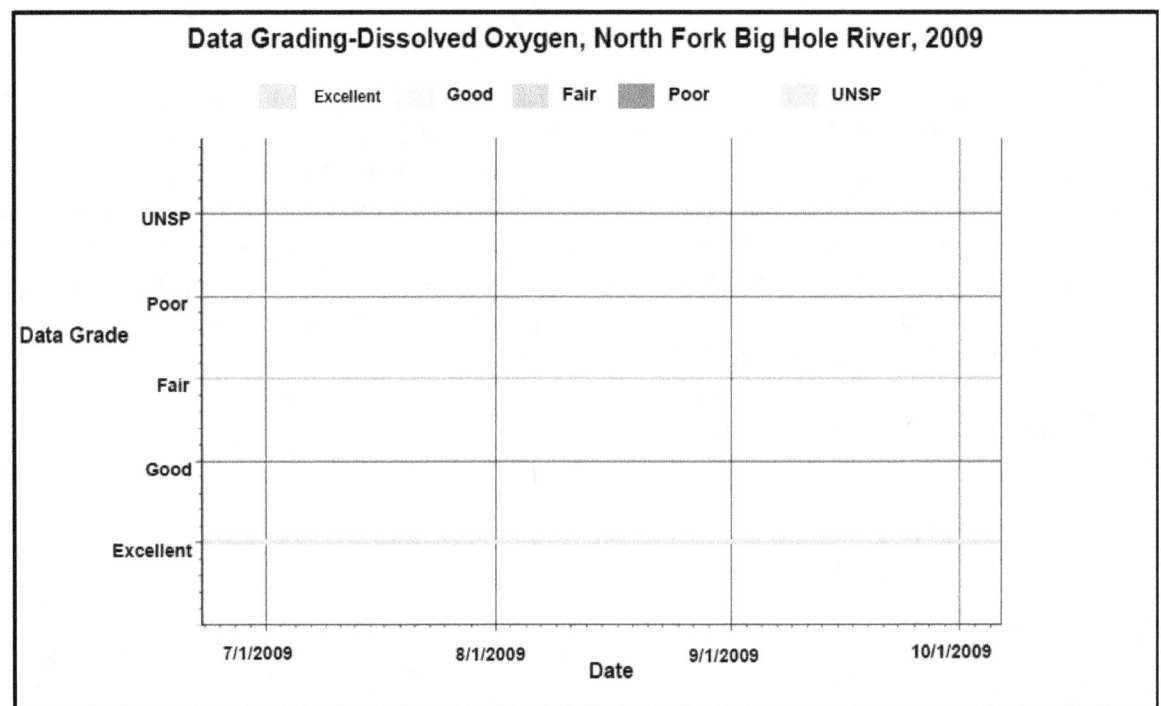

Figure 8. Data grade/rating for dissolved oxygen each deployment period June-October in North Fork Big Hole River, BIHO, 2009.

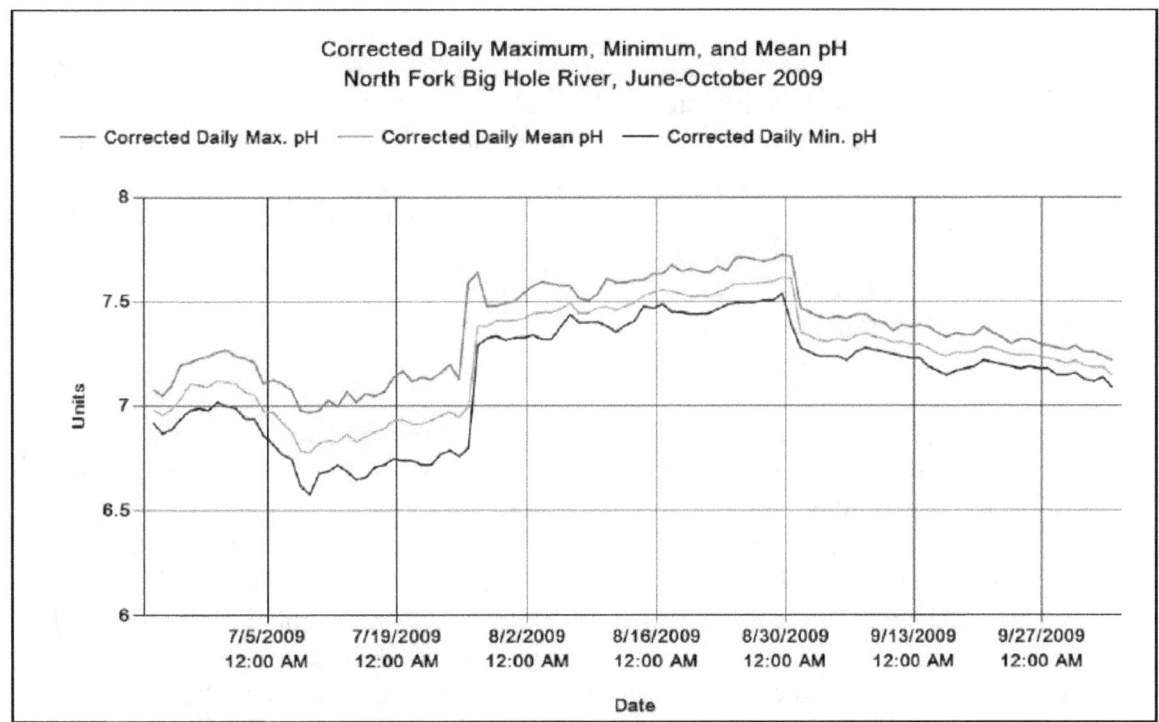

Figure 9. Corrected daily maximum, minimum, and mean pH in North Fork Big Hole River, BIHO, 2009. Note that the maximum and minimum regulatory thresholds were never exceeded (6.5, 8.5 pH units, <0.5 unit human induced change)

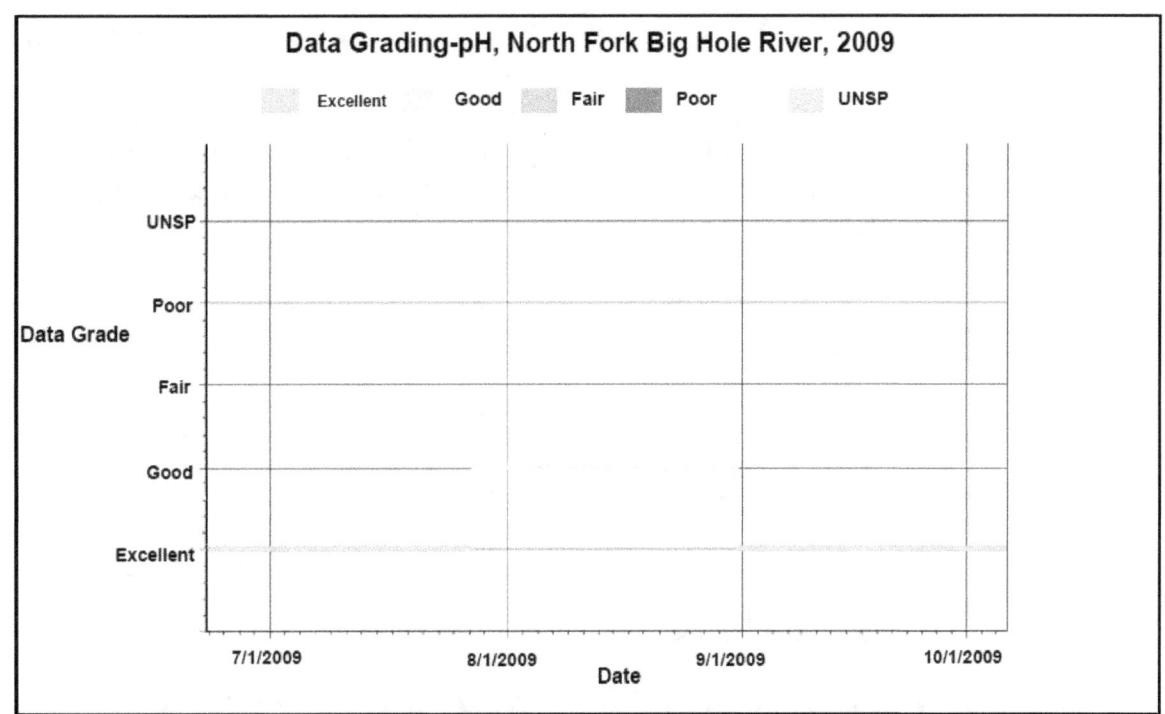

Figure 10. Data grade/rating for pH each deployment period June-October in North Fork Big Hole River, BIHO, 2009. Note that the data grade of "good" was due primarily to sensor fouling.

- Turbidity:

Prior to discussion about turbidity in the North Fork Big Hole River, it should be noted that conclusions based on this data are limited due to marginal data quality (Figure 12). Factors influencing data quality are discussed below. Regulatory thresholds for turbidity state that "no increase above natural turbidity is allowed." Our data indicates that turbidity values ranged from 0 NTU to 613 NTU. It is important to note that the method detection limit (MDL) for this sensor is 0.2 NTU and the minimum level of quantitation (ML) is 0.58 NTU (Appendix E). Figure 11 shows the daily maximum turbidity in the North Fork Big Hole River from June-October 2009. Corrections that have been applied to turbidity data are listed in Appendix F.

The spikes in turbidity seen in Figure 11 correspond to increased discharge from rain events. The two largest of these spikes were caused by substantial rainfall in the Trail Creek drainage on the area burned by the May Creek Fire in 2008 and the Rat Creek Fire in 2007. These rapid spikes in turbidity were visually confirmed during benthic macroinvertebrate sampling. Both spikes occurred shortly after re-calibration of the sensor and should be seen as a reasonably accurate picture of stream conditions. During re-calibration, the river had very low turbidity levels (< 0.58 NTU) and the following day during macroinvertebrate sample collection, a tape measure could not be seen approximately 2 cm under the water. The extremely poor data quality during the second and third deployment periods was due to sediment (primarily ash) settling out of the water column onto the sensors.

Although conclusions are limited based on the quality of data collected in 2009 it is likely that the North Fork Big Hole River does experience occasional pulses of turbidity/sediment due to recent fire activity in the watershed. These pulses are likely an infrequent event that elevated turbidity above average levels. As long as these events remain infrequent, turbidity does not appear to be a major threat to water quality in the North Fork Big Hole River.

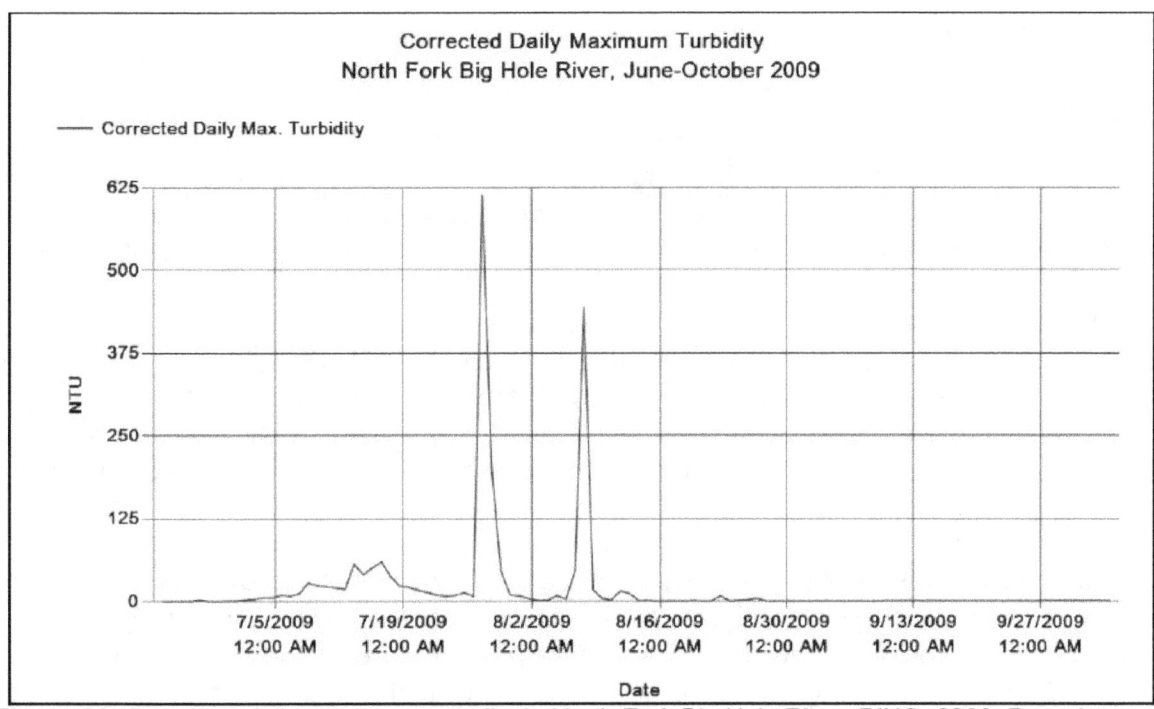

Figure 11. Corrected daily maximum turbidity in North Fork Big Hole River, BIHO, 2009. Poor data grades presented in Figure 12 suggest this turbidity data should be viewed with some caution. The state DEQ regulatory threshold for turbidity states, "no increase above natural turbidity is allowed."

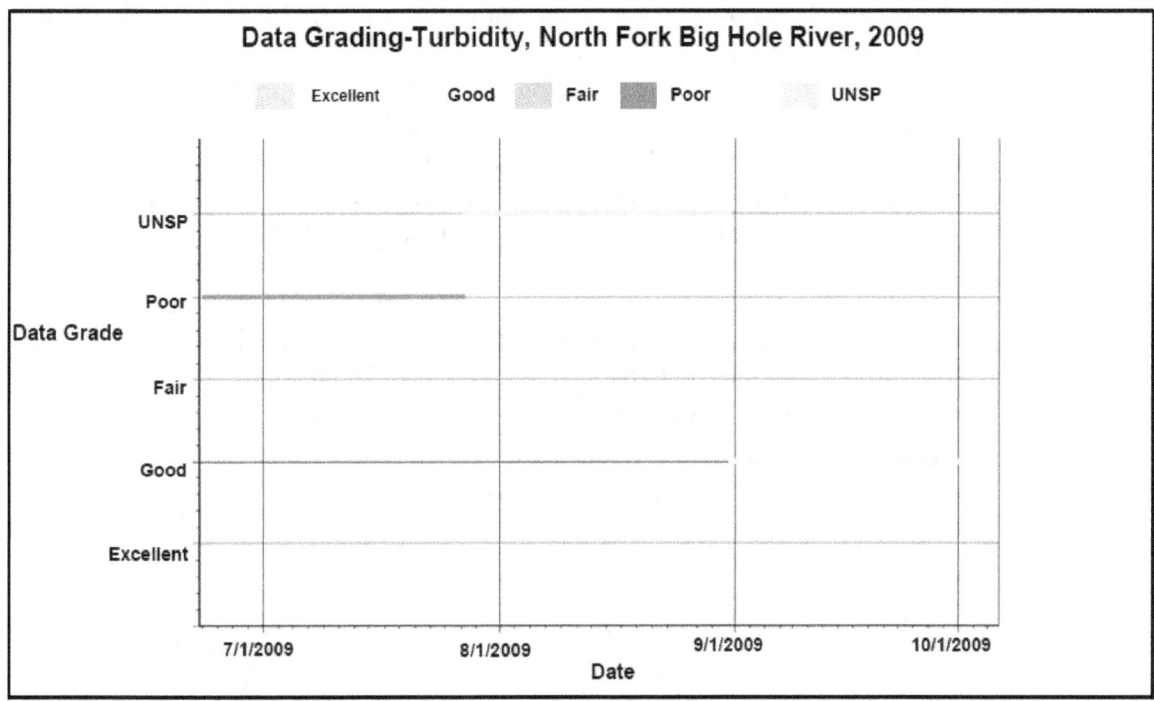

Figure 12. Data grade/rating for turbidity each deployment period June-October in North Fork Big Hole River, BIHO, 2009. Note that the poor data rating was due to the removal of a high number of outliers and UNSP (unusable) data grade was due to fouling.

Macroinvertebrates

Status:

Two macroinvertebrate metrics, the Hilsenhoff Biotic Index (HBI) and a multi-metric index (MMI), indicate "good" water quality condition (i.e., relatively unimpaired) in the North Fork Big Hole River (BIHO; Tables 2 and 3). These general status assessments are based on methods in Hilsenhoff (1987) and the Montana Department of Environmental Quality (MT DEQ 2006).

The HBI values ranged from 3.59 to 5.39 indicating that water quality is "good" to "very good" (Hilsenhoff 1987). The HBI also indicates that there may be "slight" to "some" organic pollution in the North Fork of Big Hole River (Hilsenhoff 1987). However, since the UCBN field crew collected reach-wide composite samples, and HBI values are typically calculated for samples from riffles only; the relative assessment of water quality in BIHO may be skewed to indicate lower water quality.

A multi-metric index (MMI) score was calculated according to methods outlined by MT DEQ (2006). This technique involved the rarefaction of taxa counts to 300 and the use of scoring formulas for the site class "Mountains." Results indicate that 4 of the 6 sample reaches were "un-impaired" (values ≥63), while 2 reaches were between 62 and 29 and had "moderate impairment" (MT DEQ 2006) (Table 3). The mean MMI score for all sample reaches was 66, which indicates that the segment of the North Fork Big Hole River within the park is "un-impaired." As with the HBI values, these multi-metric indices are typically calculated for samples collected in riffles. Therefore, results from sampling in 2009 may over estimate the number of impaired sample reaches.

A 2009 report on the North Fork Big Hole River by MT DEQ states that "the aquatic insect community health was below regional reference metric thresholds at both sites [n=2]" and that "community metrics do not meet thresholds based upon regional reference conditions" (MT DEQ 2009). As a result, it is reasonable to conclude that stream reaches within BIHO are potentially less impaired than the two reaches sampled by the department of environmental quality.

In the future, samples will be collected in a manner more consistent with the techniques used by the MT DEQ and other regional analysis. Proposed methods are outlined in the PACFISH/INFISH Biological Opinion (PIBO) Effectiveness Monitoring Program's Sampling Protocol for Stream Channel Attributes (Heitke et al. 2008).

Table 2. Vital sign summary table for benthic macroinvertebrates in North Fork Big Hole River, 2009. Sample reaches 1-6.

Measure	001	002	003	004	005	006	Mean
				Current Condition			
				Sample Reach			
Dominance Measures							
% Top 3 dominant taxon	31.00	24.57	23.97	43.22	31.51	25.00	29.88
Richness Measures							
Species richness	95	78	72	72	52	58	71.17
EPT richness	33	29	28	33	20	20	21.17
Community Composition							
% EPT	25.52	44.72	29.85	55.30	45.80	37.50	39.78
Functional Group Composition							
% Filterers	18.71	13.05	19.83	5.93	5.04	2.65	10.87
% Gatherers	41.40	32.05	23.53	20.55	23.11	26.14	27.80
% Predators	20.98	27.45	29.63	28.18	44.54	48.48	33.21
% Scrapers	8.88	15.93	14.81	10.59	11.34	11.74	12.22
% Shredders	8.70	10.17	9.80	34.32	15.97	7.58	14.42
Biotic Indices							
Hilsenhoff Biotic Index [HBI]	5.39	4.04	4.49	4.02	3.59	3.82	4.23

19

Table 3. Multi-metric index (MMI) for benthic macroinvertebrates in the North Fork Big Hole River, 2009. MMI calculations were based on formulas for the site class "mountains" (Montana Department of Environmental Quality 2006). "Un-impaired" reaches have an MMI score ≥ 63 and "impaired" sites <63. Montana DEQ subdivides impairment into "moderate" (62-29) and severe impairment (<29).

| | Current Condition | | | | | | |
| | Sample Reach | | | | | | |
Measure	001	002	003	004	005	006	Mean
Ephemeroptera taxa	100	100	60	80	70	100	85
Plecoptera Taxa	57	57	71	100	71	57	69
%EPT	25	48	33	61	51	42	43
%non-insects	0	64	0	54	55	53	38
%predators	51	67	79	68	100	100	77
Burrower % taxa	92	100	100	100	98	91	97
HBI	33	56	52	57	65	61	54
MMI	51	70	57	74	73	72	66
Impairment Status	Impaired	Unimpaired	Impaired	Unimpaired	Unimpaired	Unimpaired	Unimpaired

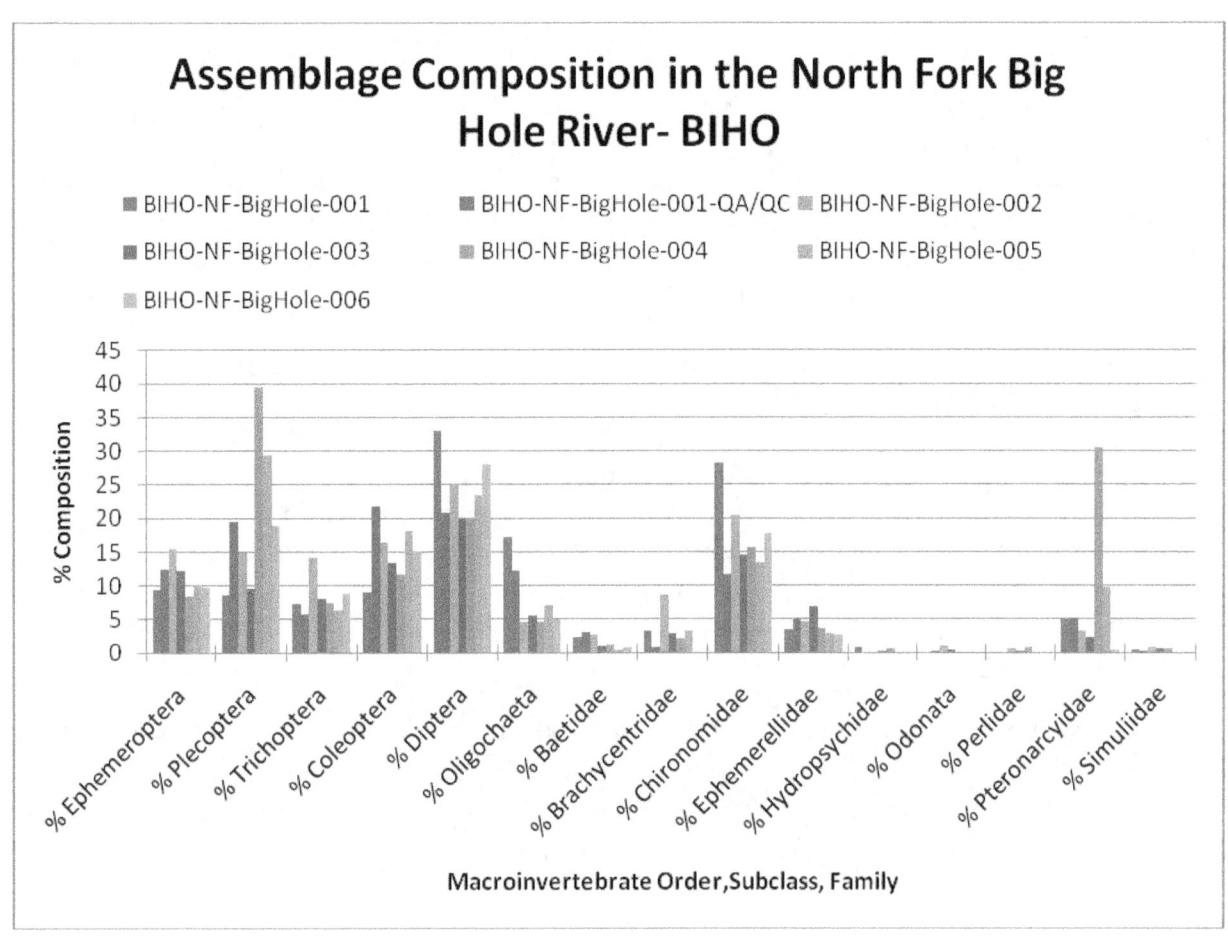

Figure 13. Percent assemblage composition in North Fork Big Hole River, 2009.

Coliform

Status:

Results of coliform sampling indicate that the North Fork Big Hole River is considered "Unimpaired" relative to Montana DEQ pathogen standard for fecal coliform prior to February 2006 (Table 4). After February 2006, the pathogen standard changed from fecal coliform to E. coli (*Escherichia coli*). Samples collected in September and October showed much lower coliform levels than those reported by WRD in their baseline water quality data inventory (NPS 1997). In August 1978 total coliform in Trail Creek was 2,060 COL/100 mL and 2,020 COL/100 mL in Elk Creek; fecal coliform levels were 209 and 200 COL/100mL respectively (NPS1997). The baseline inventory report indicates that both samples from 1978 "exceeded the WRD bathing water screening criterion of 200 CFU/100 ml (NPS1997)."

In the future, E. coli should be sampled along with or instead of coliform. Coliform and E. coli are considered of interest in BIHO due to the primary contact recreation (primarily fishing) that occurs in the river. Given that the park already conducts routine coliform sampling of its drinking water, occasional samples of stream water during the summer would be relatively easy to obtain. Intermittent samples would help establish a baseline to which future samples can be compared.

Table 4. Results of coliform samples taken in the North Fork Big Hole River in September and October 2009.

Sample Date	Location	Total Coliform	Fecal Coliform
9/01/2009	Near parking lot (downstream of bridge)	1050 COL/100 mL	Positive (*no levels reported by health dept.*)
10/07/2009	Near parking lot (downstream of bridge)	344 COL/100 mL	30 COL/100 mL
10/07/2009	Confluence of Trail and Ruby Creeks	649 COL/100 mL	22 COL/100 mL

 # COL/100 mL = # Coliform bacteria colonies per 100 mL

Literature Cited

Barbour, M. T., J. Gerritsen, B. D. Snyder, and J. B. Stribling. 1999. Rapid Bioassessment Protocols for Use in Streams and Wadeable Rivers: Periphyton, Benthic Macroinvertebrates and Fish, Second Edition. EPA 841-B-99-002. U.S. Environmental Protection Agency.

Garrett, L. K., T. J. Rodhouse, G. H. Dicus, C. C. Caudill, and M. R. Shardlow. 2007. Vitals Signs Monitoring Plan, Upper Columbia Basin Network. Natural Resource Report NPS/PWR/UCBN/NRR—2007/002. National Park Service, Fort Collins, CO.

Heitke, J. D., E. J. Archer, D. D. Dugaw, B. A. Bouwes, E. A. Archer, R. C. Henderson, J. L. Kershner. 2008. Effectiveness monitoring for streams and riparian areas: sampling protocol for stream channel attributes. PACFISH/INFISH- Biological Opinion Effectiveness Monitoroing Program (PIBO-EM). Logan, UT. (http://www.fs.fed.us/biology/fishecology/emp). Accessed 18 January 2010.

Hilsenhoff, W. L. 1987. An improved biotic index of organic stream pollution. Great Lakes Entomologist **20**:31-39.

Irwin, R. J. 2008. Draft Part B lite QA/QC review checklist for aquatic vital sign monitoring protocols and SOPs, National Park Service, Water Resources Division. Fort Collins, CO. (http://www.nature.nps.gov/water/Vital_Signs_Guidance/Guidance_Documents/PartBLite.pdf). Accessed 18 February 2010.

McCullough, D. A. 1999. A review and synthesis of effects of alterations to the water temperature regime on freshwater life stages of salmonids, with special reference to chinook salmon. EPA 910-R-99-010. U.S. Environmental Protection Agency, Washington, DC.

Montana Department of Environmental Quality (DEQ). 2006. Sample Collection, Sorting, and Taxonomic Identification of Benthic Macroinvertebrates. Water Quality Planning Bureau. Standard Operation Procedure (WQPBWQM-009). Helena, MT.

Montana Department of Environmental Quality (DEQ). 2009. Upper and North Fork Big Hole River planning area TMDLs and framework water quality restoration approach. MO3-TMDL-01A. Helena, MT.

National Park Service (NPS) 1997. Baseline water quality data inventory and analysis: Big Hole National Battlefield and Bear Paw Battlefield. NPS/NRWRD/NRTR-97/115. Fort Collins, CO.

National Park Service (NPS). 1999. Natural resource challenge: the National Park Service's action plan for preserving natural resources. US Department of the Interior National Park Service, Washington D.C. (http://www.nature.nps.gov/challenge/challengedoc/index.htm). Accessed 18 February 2010.

Peck, D. V., A. T. Herlihy, B. H. Hill, R. M. Hughes, P. R. Kaufmann, D. Klemm, J. M. Lazorchak, F. H. McCormick, S. A. Peterson, P. L. Ringold, T. Magee, and M. Cappaert. 2006. Environmental Monitoring and Assessment Program-Surface Waters Western Pilot Study: Field Operations Manual for Wadeable Streams. EPA/620/R-06/003. U.S. Environmental Protection Agency, Washington, DC.

Starkey, E. N., L. K. Garrett, T. J. Rodhouse, G. H. Dicus, and R. K. Steinhorst. 2008. Upper Columbia Basin Network integrated water quality monitoring protocol: Narrative version 1.0. Natural Resource Report NPS/UCBN/NRR—2008/026. National Park Service, Fort Collins, CO. (http://science.nature.nps.gov/im/units/ucbn/reports/index.cfm#IWQ_Mon). Accessed 18 February 2010.

United States EPA. 2001. Environmental Monitoring and Assessment Program (EMAP): National Coastal Assessment Quality Assurance Project Plan 2001-2004. United States Environmental Protection Agency, Office of Research and Development, National Health and Environmental Effects Research Laboratory, Gulf Ecology Division, Gulf Breeze, FL.EPA/620/R-01/002.

United States EPA. 1995. Environmental Monitoring and Assessment Program (EMAP): Laboratory Methods Manual-Estuaries, Volume 1: Biological and Physical Analyses. U.S. Environmental Protection Agency, Office of Research and Development , Narragansett, RI. EPA/620/R-95/008.

Vannote, R. L., and B. W. Sweeney. 1980. Geographic analysis of thermal equilibria: a conceptual model for evaluating the effect of natural and modified thermal regimes on aquatic insect communities. The American Naturalist **115:** 667–695.

Wagner, R. J., R. W. Boulger Jr., C. J. Oblinger, and B. A. Smith. 2006. Guidelines and Standard procedures for continuous water-quality monitors: station operation, record computation, and data reporting: U.S. Geological Survey Techniques and Methods 1–D3, 51.

Appendix A.
2009 Water Quality Monitoring Locations

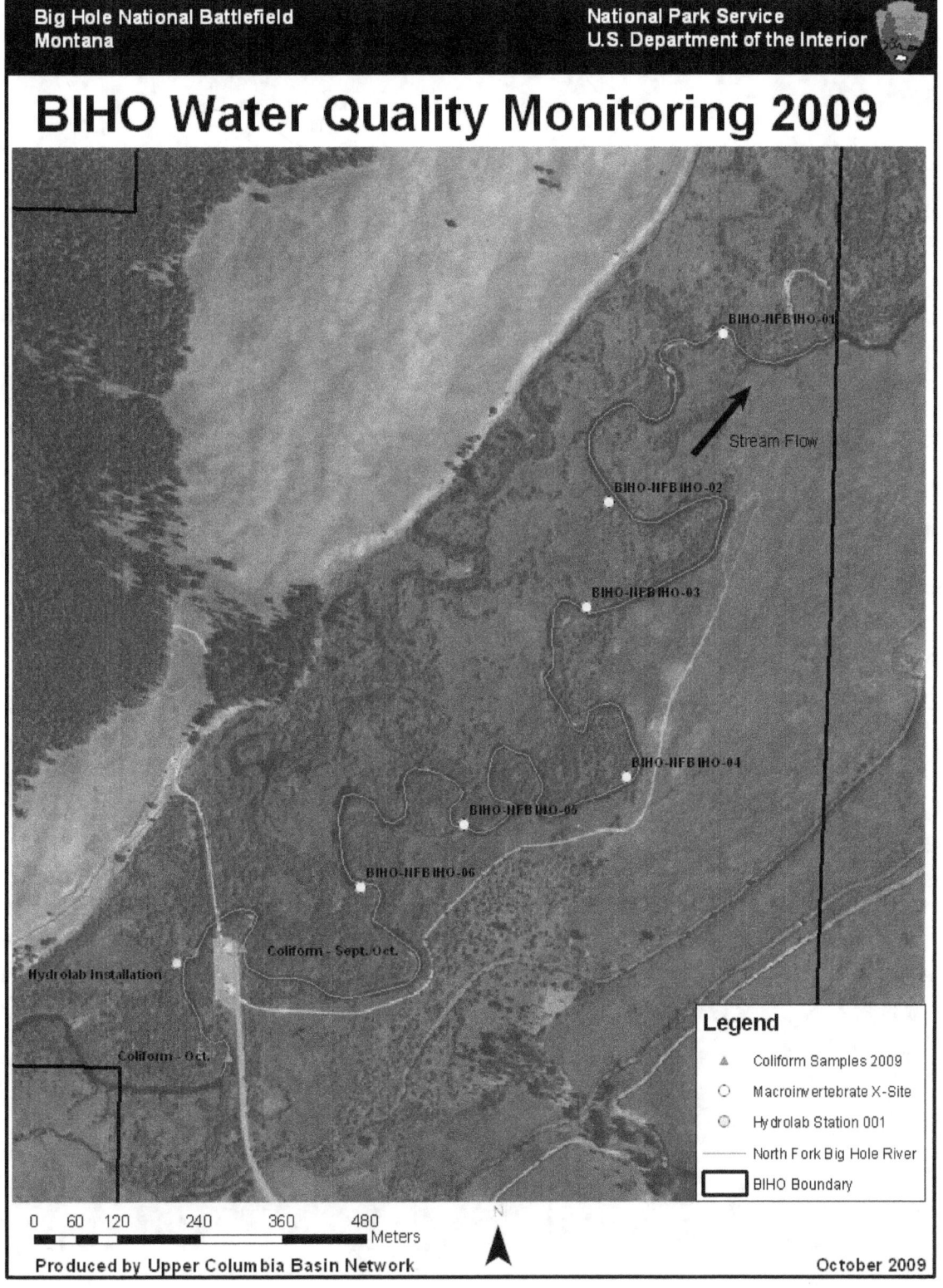

Appendix B. BIHO Hydrologic Unit Code Boundaries

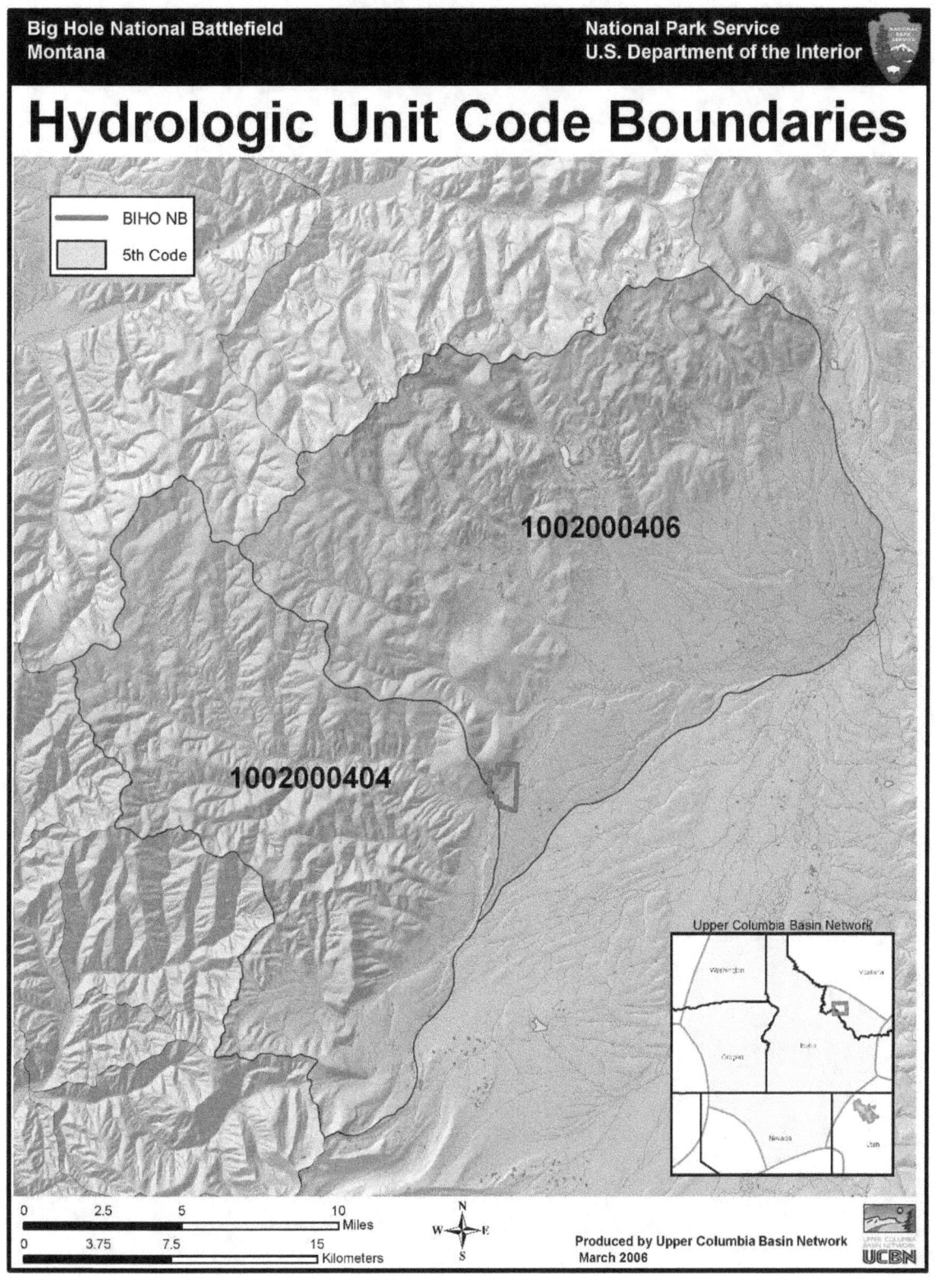

27

Appendix C. Sample Locations for Water Quality Monitoring at BIHO

Park	Stream	Monitoring Type	Macroinvertebrate Site ID	Lat.	Long.	Y	X
BIHO	North Fork Big Hole River	Macroinvertebrate	001	45.65166414	-113.64428200	5058747.22112554	293967.64787458
BIHO	North Fork Big Hole River	Macroinvertebrate	002	45.64949222	-113.64631461	5058511.15877302	293801.30198683
BIHO	North Fork Big Hole River	Macroinvertebrate	003	45.64815681	-113.64667210	5058363.71882882	293768.54303969
BIHO	North Fork Big Hole River	Macroinvertebrate	004	45.64603477	-113.64581681	5058125.76313756	293827.39705952
BIHO	North Fork Big Hole River	Macroinvertebrate	005	45.64536254	-113.64881300	5058058.79902540	293591.45506321
BIHO	North Fork Big Hole River	Macroinvertebrate	006	45.64453256	-113.65068711	5057971.42302257	293442.36506176
BIHO	North Fork Big Hole River	Water Chemistry	-	45.64349069	-113.65407131	5057864.40922562	293174.81524242

Note that X and Y have been projected in NAD 83, UTM Zone 12. These locations were recorded by the field crew with a handheld GPS unit.

Appendix D. 2009 Water Quality Photo Point Locations at BIHO

Park	Stream	Macroinvertebrate Site ID	Transect	Distance from Left Bank Permanent Marker
BIHO	North Fork Big Hole River	001	F	9.1
BIHO	North Fork Big Hole River	002	F	9.0
BIHO	North Fork Big Hole River	003	F	8.3
BIHO	North Fork Big Hole River	004	F	7.7
BIHO	North Fork Big Hole River	005	F	5.4
BIHO	North Fork Big Hole River	006	F	6.3

Photos were taken facing upstream, downstream, and of the left and right banks.

Appendix E. Quality Control (QC) Indicators

QC data quality indicators for 2009 season at BIHO, North Fork Big Hole River, Hydrolab Loaner*, Station #BIHO 001.

STORET Name	Units	Detection Range Description from Manufacture	Method Detection Limit (MDL)	Minimum Level of Quantitation (ML)	Alternative Measurement Sensitivity Plus (AMS+) Beginning of Season	Alternative Measurement Sensitivity Plus (AMS+) End of Season	Precision+ (RPD) Beginning of Season	Precision+ (RPD) End of Season
Temperature, water	deg C	-5 to 50°C	N/A	N/A	0.01	*	0.00	*
Specific Conductance	µS/cm	0 to 100,000 µS/cm	N/A	N/A	0.4	*	0.38	*
Dissolved Oxygen	mg/L	0-20 mg/L	N/A	N/A	0.03	*	0.00	*
pH	pH units	0-14 Units	N/A	N/A	0.05	*	0.14	*
Turbidity	NTU	0-3000 NTU	0.2	0.78	N/A	N/A	0.00	*

* A loaner Hydrolab was used as UCBN Hydrolab #064 was repaired. The loaner was returned to Hach during the field season and Hydrolab 064 (below) was used for the remainder of data collection.

QC data quality indicators for 2009 season at BIHO, Hydrolab 064, Station #BIHO 001.

STORET Name	Units	Detection Range Description from Manufacture	Method Detection Limit (MDL)	Minimum Level of Quantitation (ML)	Alternative Measurement Sensitivity Plus (AMS+) Beginning of Season	Alternative Measurement Sensitivity Plus (AMS+) End of Season	Precision+ (RPD) Beginning of Season	Precision+ (RPD) End of Season
Temperature, water	deg C	-5 to 50°C	N/A	N/A	0.08	0.28	0.06	0.00
Specific Conductance	µS/cm	0 to 100,000 µS/cm	N/A	N/A	0.3	0.6	0.00	0.00
Dissolved Oxygen	mg/L	0-20 mg/L	N/A	N/A	0.02	0.05	0.64	0.10
pH	pH units	0-14 Units	N/A	N/A	0.03	0.17	0.29	0.00
Turbidity	NTU	0-3000 NTU	0.2	0.58	N/A	N/A	1.85	0.00

Appendix F. Corrections History

Correction history for North Fork Big Hole River, BIHO 2009 temperature data.

Correction #	From	To	Comment
		No Corrections Applied	

Correction history for North Fork Big Hole River, BIHO 2009 specific conductance data.

Correction #	From	To	Comment
1	7/27/2009 14:00	8/31/2009 8:00	Drift Correction with Calibration Drift value of 3.850 and Fouling Drift value of -1.3 μS/cm
2	8/13/2009 20:00	8/13/2009 20:00	Delete region due to outlier
3	8/22/2009 20:00	8/22/2009 20:00	Delete region due to outlier
4	6/22/2009 15:00	7/27/2009 7:00	Drift Correction with Calibration Drift value of -10.400 and Fouling Drift value of -0.5 μS/cm

Correction history for North Fork Big Hole River, BIHO 2009 dissolved oxygen data.

Correction #	From	To	Comment
1	9/18/2009 3:00	9/18/2009 3:00	Delete region due to outlier

Correction history for North Fork Big Hole River, BIHO 2009 pH data.

Correction #	From	To	Comment
1	7/27/2009 18:00	8/31/2009 8:00	Drift Correction with Calibration Drift value of 0.060 and Fouling Drift value of 0.31 Units

Correction history for North Fork Big Hole River, BIHO 2009 turbidity data.

Correction #	From	To	Comment
1	6/24/2009 16:00	6/24/2009 16:00	Delete region due to outlier
2	6/30/2009 14:00	6/30/2009 14:00	Delete region
3	7/3/2009 4:00	7/3/2009 4:00	Delete region due to outlier
4	7/3/2009 13:00	7/3/2009 13:00	Delete region due to outlier
5	7/5/2009 0:00	7/26/2009 15:00	Drift Correction with Calibration Drift value of 0.100 and Fouling Drift value of -2.0 NTU. Pro-rated from July 5th 0:00 to July 26th 19:00 to avoid negative values
6	6/22/2009 15:00	7/27/2009 7:00	Preprocessing Horizontal Trim
7	7/27/2009 14:00	8/31/2009 8:00	Drift Correction with Calibration Drift value of 0.000 and Fouling Drift value of NTU. Drift correction should have been -5.3. This was not applied due to negative values created toward the end of the deployment. Reflected in data grade.
8	8/5/2009 21:00	8/5/2009 21:00	Delete region due to outlier
9	8/26/2009 12:00	8/26/2009 12:00	Delete region due to outlier
10	9/9/2009 19:00	9/9/2009 19:00	Delete region due to outlier
11	9/11/2009 18:00	9/11/2009 18:00	Delete region due to outlier
12	8/31/2009 14:00	10/6/2009 8:00	Drift Correction with Calibration Drift value of 0.750 and Fouling Drift value of 0.000 NTU

Appendix G. Summary Information for Each Macroinvertebrate Sample Reach

Park	Stream	Site	Date	Mean Wetted Width (m)	Sample Reach Length	Total transects sampled	% of sample taken in each substrate category:				% of sample taken in each channel type:			
							Fine	Gravel	Coarse	Hard pan	Pool	Glide	Riffle	Rapid
BIHO	North Fork Big Hole River	001	7/28/2009	11.85	300	11	27.3	63.6	9.1	0.0	18.2	63.6	18.2	0.0
BIHO	North Fork Big Hole River	002	7/28/2009	11.46	300	11	36.4	54.5	9.1	0.0	18.2	54.5	27.3	0.0
BIHO	North Fork Big Hole River	003	7/28/2009	12.71	300	11	45.5	0.0	54.5	0.0	27.3	54.5	18.2	0.0
BIHO	North Fork Big Hole River	004	7/29/2009	10.39	300	11	54.5	0.0	45.5	0.0	9.1	45.5	45.5	0.0
BIHO	North Fork Big Hole River	005	7/29/2009	7.85	300	11	63.6	9.1	27.3	0.0	0.0	72.7	27.3	0.0
BIHO	Big Hole River	006	7/28/2009	14.32	300	11	54.5	36.4	9.1	0.0	18.2	54.5	27.3	0.0

Appendix H. Macroinvertebrate Metrics

NPS Upper Columbia Basin Benthos 2009 - BIHO
Data are adjusted for subsampling and do NOT include L/R taxa

Stream	North Fork Big Hole River	North Fork Big Hole River	North Fork Big Hole River	North Fork Big Hole River	North Fork Big Hole River	North Fork Big Hole River	North Fork Big Hole River
Site	BIHO-NF-BigHole-001	BIHO-NF-BigHole-001-QA/QC	BIHO-NF-BigHole-002	BIHO-NF-BigHole-003	BIHO-NF-BigHole-004	BIHO-NF-BigHole-005	BIHO-NF-BigHole-006
Date	07-30-2009	07-30-2009	07-30-2009	07-30-2009	07-30-2009	07-30-2009	07-30-2009
Habitat	Reach-Wide	Reach-Wide	Reach-Wide	Reach-Wide	Reach-Wide	Reach-Wide	Reach-Wide
Percent Subsampled	81.30	100.00	81.30	100.00	100.00	100.00	100.00
EcoAnalysts Sample ID	5349.1-11	5349.1-12	5349.1-13	5349.1-14	5349.1-15	5349.1-16	5349.1-17
Abundance Measures							
Corrected Abundance	650.67	360.00	640.83	459.00	472.00	238.00	264.00
EPT Abundance	166.05	136.00	286.59	137.00	261.00	109.00	99.00
Dominance Measures							
Dominant Taxon	Oligochaeta	Oligochaeta	Chloroperlidae	Sphaeriidae	Pteronarcella sp.	Sweltsa sp.	Sweltsa sp.
Dominant Abundance	111.93	44.00	57.81	50.00	137.00	36.00	34.00
2nd Dominant Taxon	Tanytarsus sp.	Optioservus sp.	Optioservus sp.	Optioservus sp.	Optioservus sp.	Pteronarcella sp.	Optioservus sp.
2nd Dominant Abundance	50.43	44.00	54.12	31.00	35.00	20.00	16.00
3rd Dominant Taxon	Pisidium sp.	Chloroperlidae	Brachycentrus occidentalis	Pisidium sp.	Thienemannimyia gr. sp.	Optioservus sp.	Thienemannimyia gr. sp.
3rd Dominant Abundance	39.36	42.00	45.51	29.00	32.00	19.00	16.00
% Dominant Taxon	17.20	12.22	9.02	10.89	29.03	15.13	12.88
% 2 Dominant Taxa	24.95	24.44	17.47	17.65	36.44	23.53	18.94
% 3 Dominant Taxa	31.00	36.11	24.57	23.97	43.22	31.51	25.00

Appendix H. Macroinvertebrate Metrics (continued)

	BIHO-NF-BigHole-001	BIHO-NF-BigHole-001-QA/QC	BIHO-NF-BigHole-002	BIHO-NF-BigHole-003	BIHO-NF-BigHole-004	BIHO-NF-BigHole-005	BIHO-NF-BigHole-006
Site							
Date	07-30-2009	07-30-2009	07-30-2009	07-30-2009	07-30-2009	07-30-2009	07-30-2009
Habitat	Reach-Wide	Reach-Wide	Reach-Wide	Reach-Wide	Reach-Wide	Reach-Wide	Reach-Wide
Percent Subsampled	81.30	100.00	81.30	100.00	100.00	100.00	100.00
EcoAnalysts Sample ID	5349.1-11	5349.1-12	5349.1-13	5349.1-14	5349.1-15	5349.1-16	5349.1-17
Richness Measures							
Species Richness	95.00	70.00	78.00	72.00	72.00	52.00	58.00
EPT Richness	33.00	27.00	29.00	28.00	33.00	20.00	20.00
Ephemeroptera Richness	16.00	14.00	13.00	9.00	10.00	7.00	11.00
Plecoptera Richness	5.00	5.00	4.00	6.00	8.00	5.00	4.00
Trichoptera Richness	12.00	8.00	12.00	13.00	15.00	8.00	5.00
Chironomidae Richness	30.00	13.00	20.00	12.00	16.00	9.00	11.00
Oligochaeta Richness	1.00	1.00	1.00	1.00	1.00	1.00	1.00
Non-Chiro. Non-Olig. Richness	64.00	56.00	57.00	59.00	55.00	42.00	46.00
Rhyacophila Richness	0.00	0.00	1.00	1.00	1.00	0.00	0.00
Community Composition							
% Ephemeroptera	9.45	12.50	15.55	12.20	8.47	10.08	9.85
% Plecoptera	8.70	19.44	14.97	9.59	39.41	29.41	18.94
% Trichoptera	7.37	5.83	14.20	8.06	7.42	6.30	8.71
% EPT	25.52	37.78	44.72	29.85	55.30	45.80	37.50
% Coleoptera	9.07	21.67	16.51	13.29	11.65	18.07	15.15
% Diptera	32.89	20.83	25.14	19.83	19.92	23.53	28.03
% Oligochaeta	17.20	12.22	4.61	5.66	4.66	7.14	4.92
% Baetidae	2.27	3.06	2.69	1.09	1.27	0.42	0.76
% Brachycentridae	3.21	0.83	8.64	2.83	2.12	3.36	0.00
% Chironomidae	28.17	11.67	20.35	14.60	15.68	13.45	17.80
% Ephemerellidae	3.40	5.00	4.61	6.97	3.60	2.94	2.65
% Hydropsychidae	0.76	0.00	0.00	0.22	0.64	0.00	0.00
% Odonata	0.00	0.28	0.96	0.44	0.00	0.00	0.00
% Perlidae	0.00	0.00	0.58	0.22	0.85	0.00	0.00
% Pteronarcyidae	5.10	5.28	3.26	2.40	30.51	9.66	0.38
% Simuliidae	0.38	0.28	0.77	0.65	0.64	0.00	0.00

Appendix H. Macroinvertebrate Metrics (continued)

	BIHO-NF-BigHole-001	BIHO-NF-BigHole-001-QA/QC	BIHO-NF-BigHole-002	BIHO-NF-BigHole-003	BIHO-NF-BigHole-004	BIHO-NF-BigHole-005	BIHO-NF-BigHole-006
Site							
Date	07-30-2009	07-30-2009	07-30-2009	07-30-2009	07-30-2009	07-30-2009	07-30-2009
Habitat	Reach-Wide	Reach-Wide	Reach-Wide	Reach-Wide	Reach-Wide	Reach-Wide	Reach-Wide
Percent Subsampled	81.30	100.00	81.30	100.00	100.00	100.00	100.00
EcoAnalysts Sample ID	5349.1-11	5349.1-12	5349.1-13	5349.1-14	5349.1-15	5349.1-16	5349.1-17
Functional Group Composition							
% Filterers	18.71	5.28	13.05	19.83	5.93	5.04	2.65
% Gatherers	41.40	31.94	32.05	23.53	20.55	23.11	26.14
% Predators	20.98	33.06	27.45	29.63	28.18	44.54	48.48
% Scrapers	8.88	18.33	15.93	14.81	10.59	11.34	11.74
% Shredders	8.70	10.83	10.17	9.80	34.32	15.97	7.58
% Piercer-Herbivores	1.13	0.00	0.77	1.09	0.00	0.00	3.41
% Unclassified	0.19	0.56	0.58	1.31	0.42	0.00	0.00
Filterer Richness	9.00	6.00	7.00	6.00	8.00	5.00	2.00
Gatherer Richness	33.00	22.00	29.00	20.00	21.00	14.00	18.00
Predator Richness	31.00	22.00	20.00	25.00	23.00	17.00	20.00
Scraper Richness	8.00	11.00	9.00	6.00	8.00	6.00	8.00
Shredder Richness	10.00	8.00	8.00	8.00	10.00	10.00	8.00
Piercer-Herbivore Richness	3.00	0.00	2.00	2.00	0.00	0.00	2.00
Unclassified	1.00	1.00	3.00	5.00	2.00	0.00	0.00
Diversity/Evenness Measures							
Shannon-Weaver H' (log 10)	1.60	1.49	1.63	1.58	1.39	1.44	1.55
Shannon-Weaver H' (log 2)	5.33	4.94	5.41	5.23	4.63	4.79	5.15
Shannon-Weaver H' (log e)	3.69	3.43	3.75	3.63	3.21	3.32	3.57
Margalef's Richness	14.51	11.72	11.91	11.58	11.53	9.32	10.22
Pielou's J'	0.81	0.81	0.86	0.85	0.75	0.84	0.88
Simpson's Heterogeneity	0.95	0.94	0.97	0.96	0.90	0.95	0.96

41

Appendix H. Macroinvertebrate Metrics (continued)

	BIHO-NF-BigHole-001	BIHO-NF-BigHole-001-QA/QC	BIHO-NF-BigHole-002	BIHO-NF-BigHole-003	BIHO-NF-BigHole-004	BIHO-NF-BigHole-005	BIHO-NF-BigHole-006
Site							
Date	07-30-2009	07-30-2009	07-30-2009	07-30-2009	07-30-2009	07-30-2009	07-30-2009
Habitat	Reach-Wide	Reach-Wide	Reach-Wide	Reach-Wide	Reach-Wide	Reach-Wide	Reach-Wide
Percent Subsampled	81.30	100.00	81.30	100.00	100.00	100.00	100.00
EcoAnalysts Sample ID	5349.1-11	5349.1-12	5349.1-13	5349.1-14	5349.1-15	5349.1-16	5349.1-17
Biotic Indices							
% Indiv. w/ HBI Value	96.22	93.33	95.78	91.72	97.25	92.86	92.42
Hilsenhoff Biotic Index	5.39	4.06	4.04	4.49	4.02	3.59	3.82
% Indiv. w/ MTI Value	51.61	55.28	62.19	57.95	72.03	52.52	48.86
Metals Tolerance Index	3.33	3.10	3.01	3.12	3.53	3.37	3.27
% Indiv. w/ FSBI Value	21.74	37.78	40.12	28.76	33.26	50.00	38.64
Fine Sediment Biotic Index	122.00	108.00	89.00	97.00	135.00	100.00	67.00
FSBI - average	1.28	1.54	1.14	1.35	1.88	1.92	1.16
FSBI - weighted average	4.23	3.77	4.23	4.12	3.82	3.92	3.58
% Indiv. w/ TPM Value	41.97	60.56	63.72	48.15	69.92	63.03	52.65
Temp. Pref. Metric - average	1.78	2.24	1.83	1.96	2.33	2.23	1.79
TPM - weighted average	4.01	4.94	4.48	4.55	4.58	4.71	4.63
Karr BIBI Metrics							
Long-Lived Taxa Richness	13.00	10.00	11.00	14.00	14.00	14.00	10.00
Clinger Richness	41.00	31.00	31.00	29.00	35.00	24.00	19.00
% Clingers	42.34	50.83	56.43	37.25	61.02	51.68	33.71
Intolerant Taxa Richness	21.00	22.00	20.00	19.00	25.00	17.00	17.00
% Tolerant Individuals	17.25	13.99	7.01	10.21	7.41	11.31	12.70
% Tolerant Taxa	14.74	8.57	14.10	9.72	5.56	9.62	8.62
Coleoptera Richness	8.00	9.00	7.00	8.00	8.00	8.00	9.00

Appendix I. Macroinvertebrate Taxa List

NPS Upper Columbia Basin Benthos
2009

Data are NOT adjusted for
subsampling and include L/R taxa*

		North Fork Big Hole River	North Fork Big Hole River	North Fork Big Hole River	North Fork Big Hole River	North Fork Big Hole River	North Fork Big Hole River	North Fork Big Hole River
	Stream							
	Site	BIHO-NF-BigHole-001	BIHO-NF-BigHole-001-QA/QC	BIHO-NF-BigHole-002	BIHO-NF-BigHole-003	BIHO-NF-BigHole-004	BIHO-NF-BigHole-005	BIHO-NF-BigHole-006
	Date	07-30-2009	07-30-2009	07-30-2009	07-30-2009	07-30-2009	07-30-2009	07-30-2009
	Habitat	Reach-Wide	Reach-Wide	Reach-Wide	Reach-Wide	Reach-Wide	Reach-Wide	Reach-Wide
	Percent Subsampled	81.30	100.00	81.30	100.00	100.00	100.00	100.00
	EcoAnalysts Sample ID	5349.1-11	5349.1-12	5349.1-13	5349.1-14	5349.1-15	5349.1-16	5349.1-17
Ephemeroptera	Ameletus sp.	1	0	2	0	1	0	2
	Attenella margarita	4	9	11	12	4	5	2
	Baetidae	1	0	0	0	0	0	0
	Baetis flavistriga	1	0	0	0	0	0	0
	Baetis tricaudatus	1	3	0	1	1	1	0
	Caudatella edmundsi	1	0	0	0	0	0	0
	Centroptilum sp.	5	4	5	1	1	0	2
	Diphetor hageni	4	4	7	3	4	0	0
	Drunella coloradensis/flavilinea	0	1	0	0	0	0	0
	Drunella grandis	2	1	8	16	0	1	0
	Ecdyonurus sp.	0	0	0	0	0	2	1
	Epeorus albertae	0	1	0	0	0	0	0
	Ephemerella sp.	11	3	4	0	0	0	0
	Ephemerellidae	0	0	0	4	3	0	2

43

Appendix I. Macroinvertebrate Taxa List (continued)

		BIHO-NF-BigHole-001	BIHO-NF-BigHole-001-QA/QC	BIHO-NF-BigHole-002	BIHO-NF-BigHole-003	BIHO-NF-BigHole-004	BIHO-NF-BigHole-005	BIHO-NF-BigHole-006
Site								
Date		07-30-2009	07-30-2009	07-30-2009	07-30-2009	07-30-2009	07-30-2009	07-30-2009
Habitat		Reach-Wide	Reach-Wide	Reach-Wide	Reach-Wide	Reach-Wide	Reach-Wide	Reach-Wide
Percent Subsampled		81.30	100.00	81.30	100.00	100.00	100.00	100.00
EcoAnalysts Sample ID		5349.1-11	5349.1-12	5349.1-13	5349.1-14	5349.1-15	5349.1-16	5349.1-17
Ephemeroptera (cont)	Heptageniidae	2	2	0	0	0	0	0
	Heterocloeon sp.	0	0	2	0	0	0	0
	Leptophlebiidae *Paraleptophlebia* sp.	2	4	12	17	10	2	8
	Rhithrogena sp.	9	1	9	1	5	12	4
	Serratella tibialis	2	8	17	0	1	0	1
	Siphlonurus sp.	0	3	0	0	10	1	1
	Timpanoga hecuba	1	1	2	0	0	0	1
	Tricorythodes sp.	3	2	1	1	0	0	2
Odonata	*Aeshna* sp.	1*	0	0	0	0	0	0
	Corduliidae	0	0	0	1	0	0	0
	Ophiogomphus sp.	0	1	1	0	0	0	0
	Somatochlora sp.	0	0	5	1	0	0	0
Plecoptera	*Calineuria californica*	0	0	3	1	1	0	0
	Capniidae	1	0	0	0	0	0	0
	Chloroperlidae	15	42	47	23	4	0	0
	Hesperoperla pacifica	0	0	0	0	2	0	0
	Perlidae	0	0	0	0	2	0	0
	Perlodidae	2	2	2	1	0	0	0
	Pteronarcella sp.	27	17	17	10	137	20	0
	Pteronarcys sp.	0	2	0	0	2	0	1

44

Appendix I. Macroinvertebrate Taxa List (continued)

		BIHO-NF-BigHole-001	BIHO-NF-BigHole-001-QA/QC	BIHO-NF-BigHole-002	BIHO-NF-BigHole-003	BIHO-NF-BigHole-004	BIHO-NF-BigHole-005	BIHO-NF-BigHole-006
	Date	07-30-2009	07-30-2009	07-30-2009	07-30-2009	07-30-2009	07-30-2009	07-30-2009
	Habitat	Reach-Wide	Reach-Wide	Reach-Wide	Reach-Wide	Reach-Wide	Reach-Wide	Reach-Wide
	Percent Subsampled	81.30	100.00	81.30	100.00	100.00	100.00	100.00
	EcoAnalysts Sample ID	5349.1-11	5349.1-12	5349.1-13	5349.1-14	5349.1-15	5349.1-16	5349.1-17
Plecoptera (cont)	Skwala sp.	0	0	0	0	0	3	2
	Suwallia sp.	1	7	11	8	4	8	13
	Sweltsa sp.	0	0	0	0	30	36	34
Hemiptera	Aquarius sp.	0	0	0	0	0	0	0
	Corixidae	3	0	2	4	0	0	4
	Sigara sp.	2	0	2	1	0	0	5
Coleoptera	Agabus sp.	0	1	0	0	0	1	0
	Brychius sp.	0	0	0	3	1	2	2
	Cleptelmis addenda	0	9	15	15	7	1	1
	Colymbetes sp.	0	0	1	0	1	0	0
	Haliplus sp.	4	0	2	0	0	0	0
	Helophorus sp.	0	0	0	0	0	0	1
	Hydrophilidae	0	1	0	0	0	0	0
	Hydroporinae	5	0	0	0	0	0	0
	Hydroporus sp.	0	0	0	0	0	0	2
	Laccobius sp.	0	0	0	0	0	0	1
	Lara sp.	1	1	0	0	0	2	0
	Liodessus sp.	2	15	2	6	6	13	13
	Narpus sp.	0	1	0	1	1	0	0
	Optioservus sp.	24	44	44	31	35	19	16
	Oreodytes sp.	4	0	0	2	1	0	0

Appendix I. Macroinvertebrate Taxa List (continued)

		BIHO-NF-BigHole-001	BIHO-NF-BigHole-001-QA/QC	BIHO-NF-BigHole-002	BIHO-NF-BigHole-003	BIHO-NF-BigHole-004	BIHO-NF-BigHole-005	BIHO-NF-BigHole-006
Site	**Date**	07-30-2009	07-30-2009	07-30-2009	07-30-2009	07-30-2009	07-30-2009	07-30-2009
	Habitat	Reach-Wide	Reach-Wide	Reach-Wide	Reach-Wide	Reach-Wide	Reach-Wide	Reach-Wide
	Percent Subsampled	81.30	100.00	81.30	100.00	100.00	100.00	100.00
	EcoAnalysts Sample ID	5349.1-11	5349.1-12	5349.1-13	5349.1-14	5349.1-15	5349.1-16	5349.1-17
Coleoptera (cont.)	Stictotarsus sp.	2	1	10	2	2	1	3
	Zaitzevia sp.	6	5	12	1	1	4	1
Megaloptera	Sialis sp.	1	0	4	4	8	0	7
Diptera-Chironomidae	Ablabesmyia sp.	6	1	4	5	7	2	3
	Alotanypus sp.	0	0	0	1	0	0	0
	Brillia sp.	0	0	0	0	0	0	1
	Chironomini	1	0	0	0	0	0	1
	Chironomus sp.	1	0	14	0	0	0	0
	Cladotanytarsus sp.	2	0	0	0	1	0	0
	Corynoneura sp.	2	0	4	0	0	0	0
	Cricotopus (Nostoc.) nostocicola	4	0	2	16	0	0	0
	Cricotopus bicinctus gr.	0	0	0	0	2	0	0
	Cricotopus sp.	1	2	4	1	3	1	2
	Cryptochironomus sp.	3	0	0	0	0	0	0
	Heterotrissocladius marcidus gr.	8	2	1	6	7	5	6
	Krenopelopia sp.	0	0	0	2	0	0	0
	Larsia sp.	0	0	0	0	7	0	4
	Limnophyes sp.	0	0	0	1	0	0	0
	Macropelopia sp.	0	0	0	0	2	0	0

Appendix I. Macroinvertebrate Taxa List (continued)

	BIHO-NF-BigHole-001	BIHO-NF-BigHole-001-QA/QC	BIHO-NF-BigHole-002	BIHO-NF-BigHole-003	BIHO-NF-BigHole-004	BIHO-NF-BigHole-005	BIHO-NF-BigHole-006
Site Date	07-30-2009	07-30-2009	07-30-2009	07-30-2009	07-30-2009	07-30-2009	07-30-2009
Habitat	Reach-Wide	Reach-Wide	Reach-Wide	Reach-Wide	Reach-Wide	Reach-Wide	Reach-Wide
Percent Subsampled	81.30	100.00	81.30	100.00	100.00	100.00	100.00
EcoAnalysts Sample ID	5349.1-11	5349.1-12	5349.1-13	5349.1-14	5349.1-15	5349.1-16	5349.1-17
Diptera-Chironomidae (cont)							
Micropsectra sp.	15	6	14	2	3	3	0
Microtendipes pedellus gr.	1	0	0	0	0	0	0
Nilotanypus sp.	1	0	0	3	0	0	0
Orthocladius Complex	8	4	10	4	1	1	6
Pagastia sp.	0	0	2	0	0	0	0
Paracladopelma sp.	0	0	0	0	1	0	0
Parakiefferiella sp.	17	3	2	4	0	0	4
Paratendipes sp.	1	0	0	0	0	0	0
Pentaneura sp.	2	2	6	0	1	1	0
Pentaneurini	1	0	0	0	1	0	0
Phaenopsectra sp.	3	6	0	0	2	0	1
Polypedilum sp.	3	4	2	0	0	3	0
Potthastia gaedii gr.	0	0	1	0	0	0	0
Potthastia longimana gr.	1	0	0	0	1	0	0
Procladius sp.	5	0	7	0	0	0	0
Psectrocladius sp.	4	1	4	0	0	0	0
Radotanypus sp.	1	0	0	0	0	0	0
Rheocricotopus sp.	4	0	1	0	0	1	1
Rheotanytarsus sp.	0	0	1	0	0	0	0

Appendix I. Macroinvertebrate Taxa List (continued)

		BIHO-NF-BigHole-001	BIHO-NF-BigHole-001-QA/QC	BIHO-NF-BigHole-002	BIHO-NF-BigHole-003	BIHO-NF-BigHole-004	BIHO-NF-BigHole-005	BIHO-NF-BigHole-006
	Site							
	Date	07-30-2009	07-30-2009	07-30-2009	07-30-2009	07-30-2009	07-30-2009	07-30-2009
	Habitat	Reach-Wide	Reach-Wide	Reach-Wide	Reach-Wide	Reach-Wide	Reach-Wide	Reach-Wide
	Percent Subsampled	81.30	100.00	81.30	100.00	100.00	100.00	100.00
	EcoAnalysts Sample ID	5349.1-11	5349.1-12	5349.1-13	5349.1-14	5349.1-15	5349.1-16	5349.1-17
Diptera-Chironomidae (cont.)	Stempellinella sp.	2	0	0	0	0	0	0
	Stictochironomus sp.	2	0	0	0	0	0	0
	Synorthocladius sp.	0	0	0	1	0	0	0
	Tanytarsini	1	0	0	0	0	0	0
	Tanytarsus sp.	41	3	11	0	0	3	3
	Thienemanniella sp.	0	1	0	0	0	0	0
	Thienemannimyia gr. sp.	6	7	15	22	32	13	16
	Tvetenia bavarica gr.	2	0	0	0	3	0	0
Diptera	Atherix sp.	1	0	0	0	3	4	7
	Bezzia/Palpomyia sp.	0	1	0	0	0	0	0
	Ceratopogoninae	6	1	1	1	0	0	2
	Chelifera/Metachela sp.	0	0	1	0	0	0	0
	Dicranota sp.	0	0	1	0	0	0	0
	Dixa sp.	0	0	1	0	0	0	0
	Hemerodromia sp.	1	0	0	0	0	0	0
	Hexatoma sp.	13	27	15	18	9	11	7
	Limnophila sp.	1	0	0	0	0	0	1
	Simulium sp.	2	1	4	3	3	3	0
	Stratiomyidae	0	0	0	0	0	0	0

Appendix I. Macroinvertebrate Taxa List (continued)

		BIHO-NF-BigHole-001	BIHO-NF-BigHole-001-QA/QC	BIHO-NF-BigHole-002	BIHO-NF-BigHole-003	BIHO-NF-BigHole-004	BIHO-NF-BigHole-005	BIHO-NF-BigHole-006
Site	Date	07-30-2009	07-30-2009	07-30-2009	07-30-2009	07-30-2009	07-30-2009	07-30-2009
	Habitat	Reach-Wide	Reach-Wide	Reach-Wide	Reach-Wide	Reach-Wide	Reach-Wide	Reach-Wide
	Percent Subsampled	81.30	100.00	81.30	100.00	100.00	100.00	100.00
	EcoAnalysts Sample ID	5349.1-11	5349.1-12	5349.1-13	5349.1-14	5349.1-15	5349.1-16	5349.1-17
Diptera (cont.)	Tabanidae	1	0	3	2	4	4	6
	Tipula sp.	0	0	0	0	1	2	4
	Tipulidae	0	3	0	0	0	0	0
Trichoptera	Agapetus sp.	3	1	1	0	1	0	1
	Amiocentrus aspilus	1	0	0	0	0	0	0
	Amphicosmoecus canax	1	0	1	1	1	0	0
	Apatania sp.	4	1	0	2	1	1	0
	Arctopsyche grandis	1	0	0	1	1	0	0
	Brachycentrus americanus	0	0	0	0	1	1	0
	Brachycentrus occidentalis	16	1	37	7	6	5	0
	Ceraclea sp.	0	0	1	0	0	0	0
	Dicosmoecus atripes	1	0	0	0	0	1	0
	Glyphopsyche sp.	1	0	0	1	0	0	0
	Hydropsyche sp.	3	0	0	0	2	0	0
	Hydroptila sp.	1	0	0	0	0	0	0
	Lepidostoma sp.	5	8	18	8	6	3	7
	Limnephilidae	0	0	1	1	2	0	3
	Micrasema sp.	0	2	8	6	3	2	0
	Neophylax rickeri	0	0	1	0	1	0	0

Appendix I. Macroinvertebrate Taxa List (continued)

		BIHO-NF-BigHole-001	BIHO-NF-BigHole-001-QA/QC	BIHO-NF-BigHole-002	BIHO-NF-BigHole-003	BIHO-NF-BigHole-004	BIHO-NF-BigHole-005	BIHO-NF-BigHole-006
Site								
Date		07-30-2009	07-30-2009	07-30-2009	07-30-2009	07-30-2009	07-30-2009	07-30-2009
Habitat		Reach-Wide	Reach-Wide	Reach-Wide	Reach-Wide	Reach-Wide	Reach-Wide	Reach-Wide
Percent Subsampled		81.30	100.00	81.30	100.00	100.00	100.00	100.00
EcoAnalysts Sample ID		5349.1-11	5349.1-12	5349.1-13	5349.1-14	5349.1-15	5349.1-16	5349.1-17
Trichoptera (cont.)	*Onocosmoecus* sp.	2	0	0	2	1	1	0
	Psychoglypha sp.	0	3	2	3	4	1	11
	Rhyacophila brunnea gr.	0	0	1	3	1	0	0
	Trichoptera	0	2	0	1	0	0	0
	Uenoidae	0	0	0	0	0	0	1
	Wormaldia sp.	0	3	2	1	4	0	0
Gastropoda	Lymnaeidae	0	1	3	6	0	2	0
	Physa sp.	7	1	6	10	8	2	8
	Planorbidae	0	1	1	0	0	0	0
	Stagnicola sp.	3	2	2	4	6	1	2
Bivalvia	*Pisidium* sp.	32	6	8	29	8	2	4
	Sphaeriidae	2	5	5	50	3	1	0
Annelida	*Glossiphonia complanata*	1	1	0	0	0	2	0
	Glossiphoniidae	1	1	0	0	0	0	0
	Helobdella stagnalis	16	0	0	1	0	1	1
	Oligochaeta	91	44	24	26	22	17	13
Acari	*Atractides* sp.	2	1	4	5	2	1	2
	Hygrobates sp.	3	0	0	2	0	2	1
	Lebertia sp.	2	2	1	3	1	0	1
	Mesobates sp.	0	1	0	1	0	0	0
	Sperchon sp.	0	1	1	0	0	0	0

Appendix I. Macroinvertebrate Taxa List (continued)

		BIHO-NF-BigHole-001	BIHO-NF-BigHole-001-QA/QC	BIHO-NF-BigHole-002	BIHO-NF-BigHole-003	BIHO-NF-BigHole-004	BIHO-NF-BigHole-005	BIHO-NF-BigHole-006
	Site							
	Date	07-30-2009	07-30-2009	07-30-2009	07-30-2009	07-30-2009	07-30-2009	07-30-2009
	Habitat	Reach-Wide	Reach-Wide	Reach-Wide	Reach-Wide	Reach-Wide	Reach-Wide	Reach-Wide
	Percent Subsampled	81.30	100.00	81.30	100.00	100.00	100.00	100.00
	EcoAnalysts Sample ID	5349.1-11	5349.1-12	5349.1-13	5349.1-14	5349.1-15	5349.1-16	5349.1-17
Acari (cont.)	*Sperchonopsis* sp.	0	0	0	1	0	0	0
	Torrenticola sp.	2	2	0	12	0	0	0
Other Organisms	Nematoda	3	3	1	2	2	1	1
	Polycelis sp.	1	1	0	0	0	0	0
	Turbellaria	0	0	2	7	2	2	3
	TOTAL	530	360	521	459	472	238	264

NPS 341/101187, February 2010